Using Deming to Improve Quality in Colleges and Universities

School of Science, Management and Technologies
Edinboro University of Pennsylvania

Robert A. Cornesky, Sc. D.
Dean, School of Science, Management and Technologies

Ronald Baker, Ed.D.
Chairman, Department of Mathematics and Computer Sciences

Cathy Cavanaugh
Assistant to the Dean

William Etling, Associate Professor
Department of Mathematics and Computer Sciences

Michael Lukert, Ph.D.
Chairman, Department of Geosciences

Sam McCool
Assistant to the Dean

Brian McKay, Ph.D.
Chairman, Department of Chemistry

An-Sik Min, Ph.D.
Chairman, Department of Business Administration and Economics

Charlotte Paul, Ph.D.
Professor, Department of Nursing

Paul Thomas, Ph.D.
Chairman, Department of Biology and Health Services

David Wagner, Ph.D.
Chairman, Department of Physics and Technology

Mississippi State University

John R. Darling, Ph.D.
Provost and Vice President for Academic Affairs

378.73
U86

Using Deming to Improve Quality in Colleges and Universities

Library of Congress Cataloging-in-Publication Data

Using Deming to improve quality in colleges and universities / Robert
A. Cornesky ... [et al.].
    p.   cm.
    Includes bibliographical references (p.).
    ISBN 0-912150-13-0 : $39.95
    1. Universities and colleges—United States—Administration.
2. Deming. W. Edwards (William Edwards), 1900- Contributions in
management.   I. Cornesky, Robert.
LB2341.U83   1992
378.73—dc20

92-16611
CIP

Thanks to the following publishers for permission to reprint select passages:

W.W. Norton & Co., Inc. A. Bartlett Giamatti, *A Free and Ordered Space: The Real World of the University*, by permission of W.W. Norton & Co., Inc. ©1988, 1987, 1986, 1985, 1984, 1983, 1982, 1981, 1980, 1979, 1978, 1976 by A. Bartlett Giamatti.

Alfred A. Knopf, Inc. Tom Peters, *Thriving on Chaos: Handbook for a Management Revolution.* ©1987 by Excel, a California limited partnership. Reprinted by permission of Alfred A. Knopf, Inc.

Random House, Inc. Tom Peters and Nancy Austin, *A Passion for Excellence.* ©1985 by Tom Peters and Nancy Austin. Reprinted by permission of Random House, Inc.

The M.I.T. Press. W. Edwards Deming, *Out of the Crisis.* ©1986 by The M.I.T Press.

University of Oklahoma Press. Thomas E. Broce, *Fund Raising: The Guide to Raising Money From Private Source.* ©1979 by the University of Oklahoma Press.

Council for Advancement and Support of Education. Gary H. Quehl, Higher *Education and the Public Interest: A Report to the Campus.* ©1988.

Harper & Row Publishers, Inc. Warren Bennis and Burt Nanus, *Leaders.* ©1985.Gifford Pinchot III, *Intrapreneuring.* ©1986. Reprinted by permission of Harper & Row Publishers, Inc.

Jossey-Bass, Inc., Publishers. J.A. Centra, *Determining Faculty Effectiveness: Assessing Teaching, Research and Service for Personnel Decisions and Improvement.* ©1979. Peter Block, *The Empowered Manager.* ©1987. Reprinted by permission of Jossey-Bass, Inc., Publishers.

Fifth Printing   1992

MB

Printed in the United States of America
Library of Congress Catalog Card Number: 92-16611
ISBN: 0-912150-13-0

Magna Publications, Inc.
2718 Dryden Dr.
Madison, WI 53704
(608) 246-3580

Contents

Acknowledgments
Introduction

Acknowledgments

This material is dedicated to Foster Diebold, President, Edinboro University of Pennsylvania, who encouraged us to conceive of ways to improve the system in order to increase the quality of education.

We would also like to extend our personal thanks to Professor Elsie Deal who took the time to edit this manuscript, and to John Bolte, the Vice President for Administration and Finance, University of Central Florida for his contribution in writing the Resource Allocation Model.

It should be noted that not all of the authors agree entirely on each of the points presented in this manuscript. However, we do agree that the philosophy presented deserves to be considered as a means to increase the quality of education at institutions of higher education.

We'd also like to mention that the original idea for this book came from a conversation with Dr. Burton Witthuhn, Provost / VPAA at Western Illinois University. (RAC)

Introduction

"Knowledge is a scarce national resource...Unlike rare metals, which can not be replaced, the supply of knowledge in any field can be increased by education. Education may be formal, as in school. It may be informal, by study at home or on the job. It may be supplemented and rounded out by work and review under a master. A company must, for its very existence, make use of the store of knowledge that exists within the company and learn how to make use of help from the outside when it can be effective.

"Waste of knowledge, in the sense of failure of a company to use knowledge that is there and available for development, is even more deplorable" (Deming, p. 466, 1986).

Few doubt the genius of W. Edwards Deming. His focus on constant improvement and quality has transformed Japanese industry. Deming has outlined his philosophy by listing 14 points for managing quality and productivity. These points were designed primarily for the manufacturing sector, but apply to the service sector as well (Deming 1986).

Deming was born in Sioux City, Iowa, but he is best known in Japan where, after World War II, his advice was heeded and, as a result, helped their industries rebuild their nation.

Of all the people known for stressing quality, Deming is the pioneer. He stresses statistical process control (SPC) and a 14-point process for managers to improve quality and productivity. His approach is humanistic, and treats people as intelligent human beings who want to do a good job. Deming "hates" managers who allege workers are responsible for quality problems.

After convincing and encouraging the top mangers of Japan to produce quality items for Western consumption by using his SPC and 14-point process, the Japanese were exporting quality goods within five years. Japan, in recognition for his contribution to their economy, instituted annual Deming Prizes for contributions to quality of products and/or services. In 1960, the emperor awarded Deming the Second Order Medal of Sacred Treasure.

As administrators in a university setting, we examined Deming's points and considered how they might be applied to academia. This material presents our evaluations and conclusions.

To consider how Deming's philosophy can be applied to higher education, we must examine Deming's reference to business factors. The private sector is defined largely by the relationship between customers and suppliers, and by how the latter can use and improve production, distribution and service to increase quality and keep customers satisfied. Customer patronage is the object of competition among many firms. Each firm tries to maintain or increase market share by pleasing customers, and survival depends upon repeat business. A central point of Deming's philosophy involves viewing customers as part of the production line.

Higher education's concept of customers differs from the private sector's because in higher education there are no "repeat customers" in the traditional sense. Students, once enrolled, tend to remain until they graduate (some may leave the institution but usually not because of dissatisfaction). Alumni, once graduated, tend not to return to the same institution for additional degrees. It can be argued, though, that if alumni and current students are well satisfied with their experience, they will recommend the institution to others. Likewise, employers who are well satisfied with the university's graduates may be disposed to hire additional graduates from the university. Thus students, alumni and employers share some characteristics of traditional customers.

A further parallel to the customer concept lies in the relationships among various components of the university. For example, virtually every operating unit is a "customer" of the maintenance department. Individual academic departments are customers of the dean's office, and vice-versa. A university is a complex web of relationships where any given person or office is both a customer and a supplier. Deming's philosophy can be applied by concentrating on each unit of the university in its role as a user of systems to supply service to other units, i.e. customers.

A "system" as used in this text is an arrangement of persons, places, things and/or circumstances that either makes, facilitates or permits things to happen. The very nature of a system will determine what and how it will happen. We wish to make several points about our discussion of a "system": Knowing a system makes it possible to avoid errors by not permitting the system to try to handle something it wasn't designed to handle. By knowing what the end product or service function will be, people should be able to design and/or choose a system to produce the product or perform the necessary function(s). The system may be appropriate for performing very specific functions and inappropriate for performing even closely related functions. Although the outcomes and behavior within a system should be predictable, it's not always possible to infer the over-all system performance by examining its individual parts. Finally, it's very possible that each unit within a university might very well have efficient systems, but the systems between units may be totally incompatible.

We believe, however, that if each unit adopts the Deming philosophy, university operations will improve constantly, morale and pride of workmanship will increase, and savings will be realized that increase resources. In turn, students, alumni and employers will have more reason than ever to support the university in countless ways.

On the front page of The Chronicle of Higher Education (January 31, 1990), an article entitled "Clouded Economy Prompts Colleges to Weight Changes" said a number of colleges and universities are going to "...*make changes that borrow heavily from the transformations that swept American industry in the 1980s, when stiff foreign competition forced many corporations to streamline their operations or go under.*" Similarly, during the 1990s academic institutions will be concerned with the federal deficit and a possible recession as a result of such failures as the Federal Savings and Loan Insurance Corporation. The article supports our point of view that colleges and universities should consider Deming's 14-point process for improving quality, public acceptance and competitive positioning.

Deming's 14 points

1. Create constancy of purpose for the improvement of product and service, with the aim of becoming competitive, staying in business and providing jobs.

2. Adopt the new philosophy. We are in a new economic age. Western management must awaken to the challenge, learn their responsibilities and take on leadership for change.

3. Cease dependence on inspection to achieve quality. Eliminate the need for inspection on a mass basis by building quality into the product in the first place.

4. End the practice of awarding business on the basis of price tag alone. Move toward a single supplier for any one item on the basis of a long-term relationship of loyalty and trust. Minimize total cost by working with a single supplier.

5. Improve constantly and forever every process for planning, production and service to improve quality and productivity, and constantly decrease costs.

6. Institute training on the job.

7. Adopt and institute leadership. The aim of supervision should be to help people, machines and gadgets do a better job. Supervision of management and production workers is in need of overhaul.

8. Drive out fear so everyone can work effectively for the company.

9. Break down barriers between departments. People in research, design, sales and production must work as a team to foresee problems of production and those that may be encountered with the product or service.

10. Eliminate slogans, exhortations and targets for the work force that ask for zero defects or new levels of productivity. Such exhortations only create adversarial relationships, since the bulk of the causes of low quality and productivity belong to the system and thus lie beyond the power of the work force.

11a. Eliminate work standards (quotas) on the factory floor. Substitute leadership.

11b. Eliminate management by objectives. Eliminate management by numbers and numerical goals. Substitute leadership.

12a. Remove barriers that rob hourly workers of their right to pride of workmanship. The responsibility of supervisors must be changed from sheer numbers to quality.

12b. Remove barriers that rob people in management and engineering of their right to pride of workmanship. This means, *inter alia*, abolishment of the annual or merit rating and of management by objective.

13. Institute a vigorous program of education and self-improvement.

14. Put everybody in the company to work to accomplish the transformation. The transformation is everybody's job. (Deming 1986, p. 23)

Chapter 1:
Constancy of purpose

"The wealth of a nation depends on its people, management and government, more than on its natural resources... The United States may be today the most underdeveloped nation in the world" (Deming, p. 6).

The key word in point one is *constancy*. Constancy of purpose requires having a firmly established fundamental view of the institution's mission and adopting a long-range plan through research and innovation.

Without a long-range plan, the institution will be driven by reactions to immediate concerns and will have a tendency to squander resources and move, by default, in wayward directions. Without a clear view at a very fundamental level of what the basic character of the institution will be, individuals throughout the institution will have no map to guide them in their personal development.

There are several thousand institutions of higher education in the United States. For most of these, classroom instruction (rather than research and service) is the central mission. It's vital that faculty and staff at these institutions understand the future intent of the institution. A faculty member who has ambitious research plans may be frustrated at an institution that places little emphasis on research. Likewise, an individual with an entrepreneurial bent will likely be unhappy at an institution that sees itself as focussed primarily on internal programs and students.

Institutions should be particularly careful when planning a radical change in direction. For example, one institution we're familiar with had for years been devoted to undergraduate teaching as its central mission. However, a new president decided the institution should become a research university. Accordingly, criteria for promotion, tenure and annual salary increases were changed almost overnight. Most of the faculty, having been hired under one set of assumptions, were now mismatched with the new direction of the university. Morale suffered and frustration increased substantially.

An institution, to be able to make its character clear to existing and prospective faculty and staff, must first have a clear character. It is then important that the institution make every effort to hire individuals who are compatible with the nature of the institution. One of the most common mistakes occurs when an institution primarily devoted to teaching advertises a position as if the institution was a research university. This shows that the institution itself has not come to grips with its true nature. It also misleads prospective faculty about the nature of the position and may cause a number of excellent teaching oriented faculty simply not to apply for the job.

Between the small local colleges and the major research universities lie a number of regional comprehensive institutions. These universities usually stress teaching, but may have significant service and research missions as well. However, the relative importance of the different missions varies widely from institution to institution. Again, it is important to be candid internally about the expectations of the university. Overblown rhetoric, primarily for external consumption, can distort internal expectations. We cannot overstate the importance of having a mission that is clear and widely accepted. Such a mission confirms expectations and minimizes frustrations.

Planning

Administrators must keep their vision constantly on the future as they address routine problems. They must introduce new programs and initiatives to meet changing needs, though they must be planned for. That is, they must fit the character of the institution and address one or more of the goals of a long-range plan. New programs require both start up and ongoing resources, and these types of resources must be carefully analyzed. If new and improved programs are to be offered by present faculty and staff, the cost of retraining should be calculated and included in the long-range plan. If additional faculty or staff are to be employed, the cost of the faculty members, support staff, offices and research facilities should be calculated. Once the calculations are known, an informed decision can be made about whether the program should be implemented, and if so, when.

Of all the kinds of programs and initiatives undertaken by a college or university, curriculum development is perhaps the most important. Curriculum development requires faculty who have specialized knowledge of course content and methods of instruction. It is also important to appoint a program advisory committee, consisting of future employers of graduates, which understands the terminal competencies needed by graduates of the program. A departmental program committee, working with the department chairperson, can then develop a proposal that builds the terminal competencies and the courses into the program. The department program committee must also accept responsibility for demonstrating how the program fits the long-range plan of the institution. Any major departure from the long-range plan should be rare and require the strongest possible justification. Once a department has developed a detailed proposal, it will then fall to the higher levels of administration (dean, vice president, president) to decide whether the program should be implemented and when. If the program is to be implemented, it is the responsibility of senior administration to make sure that required resources are planned for as needed. In a university system, of course, off-campus approval might also be required before any program can be initiated. This last step may or may not involve any resource allocation — most likely depending on the scale of the program and the procedures of the particular system.

Faculty must be involved in the planning process, not just for academic programs but for virtually all institutional activities. Of course, others will be involved as well. But since faculty are usually critically involved in implementing most plans, their support is essential for success. Plans that are thrust upon faculty usually meet substantial resistance and ultimately fail. Department participation is critical if constant innovation is to be included in the plan. Participation may either be direct or through school-wide planning committees. At an institution that has a tradition of sound planning, the long-range plan becomes an important map to faculty for self-development. That is, if faculty know where the institution is headed, they can mold their individual actions to help the institution achieve its goals.

Planning is everyone's job in the institution, including the staff, however, responsibility for leadership in planning rests with the administration. Employees have a right to expect their administration to plan effectively, and the administration has a responsibility to see that planning is done at all levels. The key philosophical point here is that planning must precede action, and action must not be taken unless it is planned. During emergency conditions exceptions may arise, but these should be rare. Specifically, everyone must understand that pet projects cannot be imposed outside the planning stream. *Everyone in the institution must begin to think in terms of short- and long-range plans and action activities.*

Planning requires that every unit affected by the plan be involved in its development. In this way, every unit will have "bought into" the plan as it was developed and will be prepared to play the assigned role at the agreed upon time. Effective planning can be totally subverted if even one key unit secretly adopts the attitude that the plan is unrealistic, undesirable or unworkable. Such an attitude often becomes a self-fulfilling prophecy that dooms the plan from the beginning. When plans are repeatedly subverted, the institution-wide attitude toward planning becomes very negative, and effective planning becomes impossible.

Plans come in many forms, but all plans eventually have action activities. Some plans are general and do not have rigid timetables, whereas others are very specific and have rigid unit objectives and specific timelines. Near-term plans, in particular, are usually action activities. When action plans are completed, responsibilities must be clearly identified. This means that each individual must clearly understand his or her role and the timetable. Required resources must be available at critical times. Therefore, individuals with control of the necessary resources must be a part of the "decision meeting" that completes the action activities. Action activities without clearly defined roles, timetables and critical resources are guaranteed to produce uncertainty and frustration.

A. Bartlett Giamatti (1988, p. 44) stated *"when administrators believe themselves only managers of the public policy of the place and faculty members believe themselves alone in guarding the flame of intellectual values, when presidents and deans on one hand and members of the faculty on the other may even question whether they share the same goals, the same mission, the same hopes, then they split apart. They speak of US and THEM."* If universities and colleges had planning processes that included an active involvement of the administration *and* the faculty, a sense of collegiality would be encouraged. In addition, almost everyone would be aware of and supportive of the mission of the institution. Such joint planning endeavors would also serve as stepping stones to convey the mission statement to the public.

Many presidents complain they are overwhelmed with demands that pull them away from their offices (Quehl 1988, p. 20). If presidents were more concerned with long-range planning and resource allocation to implement a constancy of purpose for their institutions, then maybe universities would take on a leadership role for our society that they once enjoyed, and not only would the faculty more clearly understand the mission of the institution, but the public would as well.

According to Quehl (1988, p. 23), *"faculty salaries now average $35,000 a year ... they worry more about getting institutional funding for things they care about, such* *as departmental programs, space, equipment and new curricula. Our sixth sense tells us that faculty are happiest at institutions that are clear about their educational mission and deeply involve faculty in decision-making."* It appears that faculty are concerned about pride in workmanship, getting everyone involved in the process and determining the long-range mission of their institution. Apparently they are concerned about quality but are frustrated about how to achieve it.

Research

The term "research" can refer to either institutional or academic research. In the context of planning, institutional research is critical. Since planning for change will have a number of impacts, it must be based on a number of assumptions related to societal trends. The impacts and assumptions must be explicitly exposed and discussed, and where questions arise, institutional research should be able to validate assumptions and to determine impacts. For example, a new program should not be initiated on anecdotal evidence; there should be a sound basis. The resources needed by the new program should be clearly identified since the allocation of resources may affect existing programs. Before any new program is started, all personnel must be aware of the impact the new program will have on the institution's current configuration. Many educational institutions attempt to improve and update programs within the current personnel workload and without any commitment of resources. Such an approach leads to frustration.

Institutional research data should be complete, accurate and freely available to everyone, otherwise it will be useless. The free availability of information serves at least two purposes. First, when people know the facts, they are in a position to offer essential advice. They can call attention to serious flaws in a developing plan. Flaws that are identified early and corrected can prevent unnecessary expenditures. Second, freely available information creates an atmosphere of trust that's essential for effective planning and high morale. On the other hand, lack of information creates distrust.

One important goal of institutional research is to determine how various systems within the institution are functioning. Systems are generally reflected by organizational charts that presumably make the "system" visually apparent. It is, therefore, essential that organizational charts accurately reflect the system they are intended to represent. Once a system is in place, it should be allowed to work. No single person should attempt to control the system. The system produces results — unsatisfactory results should dictate changes. *System defects should be constantly sought out and eliminated.* A bad system should be replaced by a good system. The enemy of a good system is a very good system. Administrators should keep logs of how much of their time is used to solve routine problems that are "outside the system." If a significant amount of routine business must be done on the basis of personal relationships rather than within the mechanisms of the system, the system is faulty and should be corrected. Ideally, it shouldn't be necessary to work outside the system, however doing so will occasionally be necessary since not all circumstances can be foreseen.

Innovation

Successfully implementing any plan requires innovation. As Deming notes, *"innovation, the foundation of the future, can not* (sic) *thrive unless the top management have declared unshakable commitment to quality and productivity"* (p. 25).

Innovation is necessary for the vigor and vitality of the institution. It bolsters morale. It reflects current changes within society. Good, innovative ideas from employees should be welcomed. If their ideas are not given a fair hearing, creative people might leave the organization (Pinchot 1986, p. xi).

Innovation is fundamental to progress. By definition, without innovation there can be no progress. It is, therefore, important to create the conditions where innovation can flourish. The institution, from top administration to every employee, must support innovation through leadership, resource allocation and organizational structure.

Leaders should use every opportunity to encourage and reward innovation at every level of the institution. This will require a re-education of many supervisors. They must learn that innovation means failures must be accepted, and even welcomed, to achieve successes (see Point 8). They must realize that most innovations in public-service institutions are imposed on them either by outsiders or by catastrophe (Drucker 1985, p. 177).

Innovation cannot thrive without resources. Resource allocation is vital since it sends the clearest message of institutional priorities. Simply to state that innovation is encouraged, and then to fail to allocate resources, will produce cynicism, not innovation.

Pinchot (1982, p. xiii) calls innovators working within organizations "intrapreneurs." He encourages intrapreneurship within organizations and suggests the following points to encourage innovation:

1. *Clearly state your vision of the company's future so that your intrapreneurs can work on creating innovation that directly relates to the strategy of the company.*

2. *Look at every level for intrapreneurs with ideas — not for just ideas alone; an idea without someone passionate about it is sterile.*

3. *Replace red tape with responsibility.*

4. *Reward intrapreneurs with new career paths that fit their needs.*

5. *Advise managers that in the game of musical chairs caused by the removal of layers of unnecessary management, safety of a sort as well as the greatest opportunity lies in becoming an intrapreneur.*

Administrators should examine these points critically, and implement them to the extent possible within their universities.

Although it takes many forms, innovation should always have a single goal: a better educated student. The "mission" of the university should relate to the "constancy of purpose" of producing a better educated student. Each unit must ... *"constantly improve design of product and service as the consumer is the most important part of the production line"* (Deming, p. 26). The institution should be committed to constant improvement. Since education, research and service are the university's most important products, each system must consider its own impact on the student and faculty first. This doesn't mean that the system must neglect other considerations, but it does mean the system must produce a quality result in its central mission. Factors such as dollars and head count should not be the prime considerations. If the system produces a responsibly educated graduate, delivers quality service, and produces quality research, then funding, increased student applications and an enhanced reputation will result.

Administrators must never forget or neglect the quest for a well-educated graduate. All program development, retraining of personnel and resource commitment must maintain a constancy of purpose — to improve the quality of the education provided to students. The result will be a highly regarded institution.

Research and innovation may dictate a new service and a new product, and may require a variety of responses, including an improvement in teaching skills, the addition of new programs and modifying and updating equipment and facilities. New teaching skills and new technologies may be required to reach different student populations with different learning abilities. Changing technologies and a better understanding of teaching and learning styles may be required to deliver up-to-date educational experiences (Cornesky and Bolte 1986). Administration must not react to competition, but rather maintain a constancy of purpose for quality.

All supervisors must constantly undergo leadership and management development. This is extremely important for the department chairperson; the hub of the academic family. Most department chairs are promoted from the ranks of department faculty. Because of this traditional process, these individuals often have little, if any, management or leadership training. And yet in many ways the job of department chairperson is the most complex in academia. Therefore, a department chairperson should receive special training at the time of initial appointment and should continue to receive additional training periodically.

Academic quality is gained or lost in the academic department. To maintain and improve academic quality, a department must be able to respond quickly to opportunities and be free to innovate. It is, therefore, vital that the budget be decentralized to the academic department level. Although there must be accountability for the cost of producing graduates, each faculty member must remember what American industry has proven: the public wants a quality product. Imitations survive and may even thrive for a very short time, but they seldom succeed. Costs must be considered, but they should certainly not be the primary determining factor in educating human beings.

One method successfully used by institutions of higher education to establish both a long-range plan and a resource allocation procedure that uses administrative leadership and faculty input is summarized below (Cornesky and Bolte, 1986).

Developing a long-range plan

The Kabala, a marvelous Hebrew mystical book, states the only thing that is certain is change. Yet it is human nature to resist change since it disrupts the status quo. As Roy Z-M Blitzer said, *"the only person that likes change is a wet baby."*

The major reason for resisting change is that it involves uncertainty and risk. Gardner (1964, p. 44) stated: *"So stubborn are the defenses of a mature society against change that shock treatment is often required to bring about renewal. A nation will postpone critically important social changes until war or depression forces the issue."* The changemaster recognizes this resistance and uses risk, crises and creativity to effect change. The changemaster recognizes that (1) transformation cannot be dictated, only facilitated; (2) the past cannot define the future, although the past may contribute significantly to the future; and (3) although we cannot influence societal values and trends and their eventual impact upon our institutions, we can, if we have a long-range plan, influence our methods of response to the trends.

The main purpose of having a long-range plan is to help us let go of the past and present and travel into the future more confidently. The long-range plan should not define the future; it should only act as a guide to how we will respond to changing events that will probably have an impact upon our institutions.

Long-range planning for academic institutions should be done in a matter of weeks or months, rather than a year or more. To condense the long-range planning process, several assumptions have to be made:

- The main responsibility for the initial phases of planning must lie with the academic division of the institution, since instruction is the central reason for any college or university to exist.
- Recognizing departmental strengths and weaknesses is best done by the members of the department, not by outsiders.
- Department chairs are the center of activity within the university.
- Administrators (presidents, provosts and deans) have inherited the past. While they can do very little to influence the route their institution will take in the short term, they can influence significant change in the long term by allocating resources that will drive the plan.

In developing an institutional long-range plan there might be three working units: one unit will reflect the input of the faculty who will define the majors; one unit will reflect the input of the department chairs, assistant and associate deans and directors; and one unit will reflect the input of administrators. Departments dealing with resource allocation/reallocation, space allotments, student affairs, security, etc. *should not* be included. The over-specification of resources in the germinal phase of planning can only stifle creativity and innovation. Resource allocation, whether formula driven or not, can be adapted to encourage change *after* the plan is accepted. The planning process should involve several feedback cycles between and among groups. The entire planning process, including the writing of the long-range planning document, should take no more than 20 working days over a 4 week period, although in large institutions, this process may take twice as long. Upon completion of the planning process, a case statement can be compiled easily in preparation for a capital fund drive.

Essential to the success of institutional long-range planning is the participation of and interaction between the academic units (faculty); the collegial units (department chairs, directors, assistant deans); and the administrative units (deans, vice presidents of academic affairs, provosts and presidents). Each unit must determine its strengths and weaknesses. It is recommended that each group have a facilitator who is not part of the institutional planning process to record the perceived strengths and weaknesses. The perceived strengths and weaknesses of each group must be shared.

With unit strengths and weaknesses identified, it is then necessary to identify societal trends that will likely affect the institution. Fortunately, societal trends can usually be recognized and their potential effects can be anticipated with some accuracy for five to 10 years into the future. The following trend areas should be examined:

- Population
- Participation
- Science and Technology
- Continuing Education

- Economy
- Lifestyle
- Government

In discussing societal trends, consider any additional trends that may be germane to the institution, i.e. those that may have an impact on policy planning and management of change.

Consider how the population trend will affect your academic institution over the next decade and reflect upon the following:

- Is the population growing, declining or remaining stable in your service region?
- What age group does your institution presently serve?
- Does your unit respond to the educational needs of older students?
- Does your institution offer degrees/courses off-campus?
- Does your institution offer courses for the over-65 age group?
- Does your institution make it possible for students to obtain degrees during the evening hours so that part-time, working students can attend?
- Does your institution use local retirees as adjunct professors?

Marilyn Ferguson, in her book The Aquarian Conspiracy, stated: "*Two hundred years ago the major public issue in the United States was the freedom from political bondage; a century later the Civil War was fought for the freedom from physical bondage; today, the issue is to be free in one's body, mind and feelings.*" Today, people are becoming more participative, rather than submitting to hierarchical structures. This results in an organic social organization. As our society truly approaches equalitarianism during the next 50 years, the demand for liberal education and computerized information retrieval procedures will increase substantially since people will grapple with questions relating to their society, work place, school districts, city management, churches, economics, etc.

People are seeking more rights in deciding about their health care and treatment. No longer is the physician's concept of health care unquestioned. Patients are demanding access to their medical records. Corporations are seeking more rights to expand into business endeavors that were previously under the auspices of others: the telecommunications system is no long under the total control of AT&T; private corporations develop their own health maintenance organizations and preferred provider organizations; stock brokers, banks and savings and loan companies offer competing services. These are but a few examples of how people and organizations influence the outcomes of their own decisions.

When looking at the participation trend, reflect upon the following:

- Do your curriculum and/or teaching methods encourage students to think for themselves and to participate actively in the learning process?
- Does your curriculum address the ethical implications of technological advances on social change?
- Do your academic departments offer seminars or courses that address international issues?
- Do your academic departments assess their contributions to leisure, equality and planning for change and freedom?

The United States is moving toward an information-based economy. The knowledge industry will influence our entire society, since it will employ 60 percent of the population. However, since scientific and technological advances will impact society immediately, there will be a growing trend to humanize a technological world.

Advances in the communications industry are phenomenal. Satellite uplinks with the C-band and the newer, more powerful Ku-band are being improved and expanded with every U.S. space shuttle mission. Two-way interactive television using computer technology and VCR's will be used extensively as several National Television Universities begin to teach courses resulting in degrees from art to zoology. Quality control issues are already being addressed.

The computer is becoming common. Each member of our society will have to be computer literate to maintain an average quality of life. All elementary, secondary and college students will be required to purchase personal computers during their educational process, much as they are required to purchase books.

As the communications industry will replace the need for extensive travel and the need for many of the polluting industries, the supply of energy should be greater than the demand. The cost of energy should thus remain relatively constant over the coming decade, especially as technological advances occur in solar, wind and wave energies.

The American farming industry will continue to be a major supplier of food for the entire world. American farmers will lease their land to foreign countries unable to produce enough food for their own people: Russia, Egypt, Japan, Kuwait, etc. The number of small, family-owned farms will decrease substantially as the number of corporate farms increases.

Chemical disposal will continue to be a major problem and, because of past practices, water supplies in many areas will be unfit for consumption.

Advances in medical technologies and medical genetics will require highly specialized professionals in bioengineering, computer sciences and the health sciences.

Concerning science and technology trends, colleges should consider:
- Are advances in science and technology affecting your region significantly, e.g. the robotics industry in Detroit?
- The half-life of scientific knowledge is two to four years, i.e. one-half of all science is either replaced or modified every two to four years. Should your institution try to remain current in the sciences or should it relegate the task of teaching science to area research-based universities?
- As a result of the knowledge explosion, the Ph.D. may become the entry level degree for engineering, computer science, nursing and the health professions. What role should liberal learning have in the educational process?
- In light of the rapid scientific and technological advances, of what value would it be, if any, to reorganize the majors in your institution? For example, should the ecology major be removed from the biology department and placed in the political science department?
- Does your institution acknowledge that if technology runs far ahead of social and organizational innovations the technology may be dysfunctional?
- Should the business college offer a graduate degree in nursing administration?

- What unique combinations can your institution offer to higher education and to society?
- Are your professional programs strong while your liberal arts and humanities programs are weak?

With the rapid expansion of knowledge, people will require and demand continuous education if they are to make informed choices in a participatory society. Since the rapid advances in science and technology will cause over-specialization, our society will have a tendency to spawn Towers of Babel. Seminar and workshop format courses, many by interactive television, will be demanded from each institution. And certificate programs will rapidly gain in popularity since they'll provide the specialized skills previous graduates will require to remain employable.

Most people realize that lifelong education and retraining will be a part of living. The entire idea of what constitutes education will be the revolution for the next 20 to 50 years.

The U.S. population is becoming more educated, with nearly 27 million Americans over age 25 being college educated as of 1984, a 2 percent increase since 1980. From 1980 to 1984, the percentage of 25- to 34-year olds with four or more years of college rose from 23.3 percent to 24.4 percent; the age group 35-44, from 19.5 percent to 25.3 percent; 45-54, from 14.9 percent to 17.6 percent; 55-64, from 10.9 percent to 14.1 percent; and 65 and over from 8.3 percent to 9.4 percent.

Universities and industries are entering into exciting partnerships resulting in a new concept of education: university on-the-job. Courses, skills and content are being taught by telecommunications as well as traditional means. University research is putting "state-of-the-art" knowledge into the "hi-tech" products we use as consumers.

Looking at continuing education, colleges should ask:
- If technological and scientific advances continue at the projected rate, it's possible that the graduates of most science-based programs (biology, chemistry, physics, nursing, medicine, allied health, computer science, engineering, etc.) could become obsolete upon graduation. How would you ensure the competency of the graduates under such a rapid expansion of knowledge?
- Is your institution considering an educational merger with an industry?

Technology leads to a worldwide economy

Sophisticated technology will lead us into a knowledge-based, worldwide economy. As a result, less than 20 percent of our population will be involved in the production of goods, while the other 80 percent will provide services. The knowledge-based economy will require more advanced education.

The world-wide economy is influenced greatly by a number of events: the transformation of a society from one base to another, the strength of a given currency, trade agreements, etc. For example, in 1985, automobiles from Yugoslavia and Korea cost less than $4,000 in the U.S. market. These prices not only affected our automobile industry but those of Japan and Germany. Manufacturers of televisions, VCR's, cameras, textiles, etc. are being forced out of business with the steady influx of foreign products. Recovery of our ailing agricultural system is still possible if export restrictions for the American farmer are modified.

The economy, however, will vary within the United States, with the South and Southwest experiencing a stronger growth than the Northeast and Midwest.

However, an international incident such as a war in the Middle East, could greatly increase the interdependence not only of our economy, but of the world as well.

The average price of a new, single-family home in 1984 was $86,100 in the South, $106,200 in the Northeast, $107,800 in the Midwest, and $109,400 in the West. Not only are the prices of new homes and fuel bills lower in the South, but so is the average disposable income. However, there is every reason to believe that with the relocation of the hi-tech industries to the southern states there will be a substantial increase in wages.

Concerning economic trends, academic institutions should look at:
- Will you be able to guide the transition from the industrial phase to the post-industrial phase?
- How will you serve various groups if the regional economy in your service area declines? Stays the same? Expands?
- What is the economic profile of your student population? How will substantial reductions in student aid affect your student population?
- Can you implement a private, for profit, business enterprise whose funds would be directed back into your budget? If yes, what would the enterprise be? How much profit could be expected? Where would the money be directed?
- What revenue-generating possibilities (e.g. businesses, grants, consulting, capital fund drives) could/should you become involved in if your institution is in financial trouble?

With the emergence of an information economy, more women will enter the work force with pay comparable to that of men. As a result, women will experience greater economic independence and personal freedom. To effect this change, women will require more education — especially at times convenient for older working women: part-time evening curriculums; certificate programs in disciplines related to the knowledge industry.

Other minorities will seek advancement based on the freedom and opportunities the information economy will provide. Like women, these minorities will require educational opportunities at times convenient for the full-time employed individual.

As American society begins to shift to a participative, egalitarian society, most of the population will have substantially more leisure time. One of the projected outcomes of leisure time will be the search for self-fulfillment. Higher education will be expected to provide a wide range of educational experiences, i.e. from spiritual perspectives to economic perspectives to ethical perspectives.

When considering how lifestyle trends will affect your institution, consider:
- Does your institution offer courses, degrees or certificates during times convenient for the population in your service area?
- Is your curriculum relevant to society's increase in leisure time? Do your professors explain its relevance?
- Can your academic majors be delivered by telecourses or other innovative means to places not readily accessible by traditional lecture/laboratory delivery modes?
- What certificate programs, if any, could your department deliver to college graduates seeking employable skills?

The federal government is decentralizing and delegating more responsibility to state governments. By the same token, state governments are delegating many responsibilities to local governments, many of which are in small rural towns that have sprung up at the expense of decaying industrial cities. There are, however, issues that most people wish to see the federal government handle, e.g. social security and environmental safety.

Since the power to make political decisions affecting higher education is shifting from the national government to the state and local governments, the health of many institutions may be related directly to how they respond to the needs of their service population.

Look at the following when considering governmental trends:
- Does your institution have sufficient support in your service region to influence favorable legislation?
- Do your state and local representatives know of the contributions your institution makes to its citizens?

A matrix should be established that matches department strengths and weaknesses along one axis with societal trends along a second axis. On the matrix, institutions should state the planned response to the challenges or opportunities posed by the intersection of its strengths and weaknesses with the societal trends. This will lead naturally to a set of goals that the unit proposes to guide its future direction and actions. Units must then share and discuss their initial planning results with other units. A series of interactions must occur where discussions are held, plans are amended and more discussions are held.

The planning process should yield a large amount of information from the three types of units, namely, the departments (programs, majors), the colleges (schools, divisions), and the administration. At this point, the level of frustration will probably be high since any dialogue regarding projections into the future will cause everyone to realize that impending change will disrupt the status quo. Furthermore, the discussions in each group and between units will usually have resulted in some sort of a compromise that should be reflected in the suggested objectives. The compromises usually leave the participants a little ruffled and wondering if anything is going to happen as a result of this effort. It is imperative, therefore, that the data be collected, analyzed and published as soon as possible. This is part of the function of the long-range plan (LRP) writing committee. The membership of the LRP writing committee is, therefore, very important.

The committee should be charged to write either a general plan or a detailed plan for the institution. In institutions with over 4,000 students, we recommend a general institutional plan with each college and department being charged with producing a detailed plan in response to the institutional plan. In smaller institutions, a single, detailed long-range plan is possible, especially if the institution is limited in its academic offerings. If there is any doubt among committee members about which plan is most appropriate for their institution, a more generalized institutional plan should be written and supplemented by more detailed, specific collegial and departmental implementation plans.

The outside-in planning process is a very effective tool for analyzing how societal trends and values will probably affect one's institution. Briefly, the outside-in planning technique is a procedure through which one analyzes an issue or trend from a global perspective to a specific internal perspective. This process is recommended to the writing committee as it begins the difficult task of writing the plan using the information generated by the unit.

If a university has an established mission or is part of a system that establishes the missions of each institution, the administration might set broad objectives concerning instruction, research, service and leadership. The academic departments might use the above described technique to determine the action objectives necessary to accomplish the mission. In either case, the faculty will have had considerable input into the plan.

Developing a formula-driven budget

By John R. Bolte, vice president for administration & finance, University of Central Florida

To drive a long-range plan, institutions may find it helpful to design a formula-driven budget that reflects the action objectives of the plan. Note, however, that formula-driven budgets can be improperly designed and used. Care must be taken to avoid certain pitfalls, some of which are described under Deming's Point 11: *Eliminate quotas and numerical goals; substitute leadership.* The following paragraphs describe commonly used budgeting processes and outline the development of a properly designed and tested formula-based budgeting procedure.

In recent years, the concerns of accountability, the leveling or decline in enrollments, and the availability of computerized management information systems in higher education have focused attention on the need for more precise and sensitive methods of providing appropriate internal resource allocation. Simultaneously, the control of internal resources in educational institutions, particularly those used by the academic areas, has shifted to individuals who are most directly involved in the use of the resources. Active involvement of academic resource users and decision makers in the allocation process has made the development of realistic allocation models possible. It has also placed additional responsibilities on offices of institutional research where data to support the allocation process should be available.

The budgeting and allocation of personnel and financial resources are time consuming and costly. Further, the number of procedures used to request and allocate resources is apparently limited only by the number of post secondary institutions in existence. Procedures range from complex and ill-defined requests and allocation methods involving several administrative levels to singular, if not dictatorial, decisions on resource allocation. Budget requests and allocation procedures also range from those requiring mountains of paperwork, historical data and rambling justifications to allocations that are purely formula-generated and based on some general variable such as student credit hour productivity.

The development and use of resource allocation models must be looked upon as a management tool. It is not a substitute for decision making. Used properly, the resource allocation model reflects policy decisions of university administrators, provides information for short and long-range planning, and has a substantial and desirable impact on the decisions made by deans and department chairpersons in the day-to-day operation of educational institutions. Used improperly, an allocation model may become a substitute for decision making and result in decisions not in the best interest of the institution. In addition, a model that's not built on a firm rational basis places the academic administrator in a continually defensive position and may create morale problems with the resource users. In general, the development of resource allocation models requires more planning and analysis on the part of the academic decision makers and therefore can facilitate an equitable and consistent allocation of available resources.

The following comments summarize a variety of procedures used in requesting and allocating resources, and describe some of the limitations and advantages of each. The list isn't complete, but it does describe procedures used in most institutions.

The Blue Sky request

Most university budget officers and top- and middle-level administrators have, at one time, experienced a budget process where unit heads with budget responsibility have been asked to submit a listing of their budget needs for a subsequent year, complete with written justifications for each item. Refinements include requiring that requests be listed in priority order and placing a limit on total dollars that can be requested. Regardless of the constraints placed on such requests, budget officers can usually expect to receive personnel requests two to five times higher, and financial requests five to 10 times higher than even the most optimistic observers would predict for available resources. The corresponding justifications for the resources range from meaningful to senseless. Only occasionally do they provide sufficient information for the inevitable judgements that must be made when the actual budgetary resources become known and available. The results of this budget approach are easily enumerated and generally negative:

- High expectations of unit heads fail to materialize, and over time these individuals become demoralized or find the whole process to be something of a bureaucratic joke.
- The process offers little in the way of guidelines for inevitable cuts in the budget requests. Did each unit head inflate his or her request equally? Should the writers of a well-written and innovative justification be rewarded?
- The volume of paperwork and extent of staff, faculty and administrative effort required to produce a budget request can be enormous.
- In what may be a more positive vein, input to the budget process seems to involve many people. At least, many people have had the opportunity to think about and provide input to the budget request process, even if their chances of receiving the requested funding are slim or nonexistent.

However, if this planning process is used, people will have had a great deal of input in determining the goals and objectives of their units. If the purpose of resource allocation is to drive the plan, then both faculty and administrators will have had input into the allocation.

Overall, the "Blue Sky" budget request and allocation procedure wastes time, deals in non-realities, and lowers the morale of participants who take the system seriously.

Planned Programmed Budgeting

"Planned Programmed Budgeting," as the name implies, requires the development of a budgeting plan for the future. In a college or university, plans would be developed in each major program category and would include cost estimates and budget requirements to complete the stated plan. Budget managers expect to receive the required funding and, in turn, are expected to complete the stated plan within the approved budget. Unfortunately, college administrators aren't known for their success in long-range planning and are even less adept at establishing realistic cost estimates for the tasks required by a plan. A complex combination of inabilities to do long-range planning, estimate student demand and enrollment by discipline, and estimate program or project costs tends to render "Planned Programmed Budgeting" useless in most colleges and universities.

Zero-based budgeting

"Zero-Based Budgeting" implies that during each budget cycle, the various budgetary units begin by assuming they have no continuing resources and that the new budget must be developed by stating and justifying each activity that will requires funding. The task can be long and laborious, but budget managers soon learn to use a previous year's budget request, adjusting dates appropriately and raising all budget figures by 2-5 percent greater than the highest available inflation estimate. Additional amounts are then added to fund new programs that are deemed to be desperately needed, or to properly fund existing programs which have obviously been underfunded (although successful) for several years. The procedure is supposed to force each budgetary unit manager to review needs and priorities periodically and thereby prevent outdated or inefficient programs from being continued. Colleges and universities, however, are people intensive, and any significant change in priorities or workload will impact personnel. A downward change may be compounded by the fact that some personnel are tenured, and administrators have limited flexibility to reduce or terminate programs. "Zero-Based Budgeting" in its true form is probably never used in colleges and universities. However, a modified procedure that's often used establishes some fixed baseline, and all expenditures in excess of this figure are specifically requested and justified. In either case, the system requires extensive and detailed documentation by administrators and budget managers. Unfortunately the documentation can seldom be used effectively when actual budgets are received and internal allocations made.

Colleges and universities operate under remarkably stable conditions in terms of workload and funding. Variations in excess of 10 percent in any one year are exceptions and almost always predictable. From a budgeting point of view, it cannot, therefore, be said that major variations in workload or funding will significantly affect internal priorities for budgeting and allocation of resources in the short term. Instead variations will affect budgeting and allocation of resources over three, five and 10 years.

With reasonably stable and predictable resources, and with the equally reasonable assumption that internal priorities do not change radically over short periods of time, the internal allocation of resources can be accomplished in a much more efficient and systematic manner, even if the purpose of the allocation is to drive the long-range plan. There is no apparent reason for administrators to request and justify budgets in advance. It makes little sense to have individual unit managers compete for reasonably fixed and limited resources through time consuming and generally unsuccessful request and justification procedures.

A more rational approach is to devote time and effort during the mid-year lull in the annual budgeting cycle to establish and agree upon allocation procedures *regardless* of total funding received, and in light of the goals of the institutional long-range plan. Such procedures can always be reduced to mathematical formulations that are easy to understand and efficient to use. The development of such a system has a number of advantages:

- The procedure provides ample opportunity to involve affected administrators and budget managers in the allocation process.
- It emphasizes the equitable allocation of available resources rather than "blue sky" requests and detailed justifications for non-existent funding.
- After funding is known, allocations can be made quickly and with few hurried decisions.
- Implementation of and changes in short- and long-range plans are still possible, but in a more realistic context for estimating available resources. Total workload and financial resources are predictable with reasonable accuracy, and good estimates of future funding in a college or department become possible using the established allocation procedures, even if the allocations are used to implement change.
- Special program emphasis over a sustained period is possible by establishing predetermined favorable allocation parameters that are known and understood by those receiving added support, as well as those who don't receive such support. Actually, these allocation parameters come from the institution's long-range plan.

Of course not all internal resource allocations can be handled by the formula approach described above. There are often legitimate and justifiable reasons for short-term special allocations. For example, new programs may require start-up funding, expensive research instruments, matching funds for a significant grant or donation, or an expenditure which will benefit all budgetary units. There seems to be no established rule for the amount of funds which should be administratively reserved for special requirements. In institutions of higher education, it is probable that administered special allocations should be equal to or less than 1 percent of the total institutional budget. Administered special allocations in an institution of 10,000 students with a $25 million budget would then amount to as much as $250,000 across all budgetary units. At best, the 1 percent figure is a rule of thumb and will depend to some extent on internal problems and future planning needs as viewed by high-level administrators. If drastic changes for the institution are anticipated over the next few years, 5 to 10 percent of the budget may have to be placed in the special allocation category.

A number of factors play a role in the development of successful allocation resource models. Regardless of the kind of resources being allocated or complexities in the use of available resources, the following factors apply:

- The model must reflect the goals in the institutional long-range plan and corresponding policy decisions.
- The model must reflect actual resource use.
- The model must be based on general factors.
- The model must be more complex and detailed when resources are allocated close to the administrative level where they will be used.
- The model must be adaptable to mathematical formulation that is easily understood by resource users.

The model must reflect previously established institutional goals and policy decisions as reflected in the long-range plan. More important, the model must be designed and stated so it encourages the attainment of institutional goals. For example, an allocation model might reflect an institutional goal to emphasize and build a strong fine arts program by providing favorable allocation parameters in this area. Similarly, if institutional administrators feel strongly that faculty travel to professional meetings is important to the growth and development of the institution, the allocation model should specifically identify professional travel as an allocation category. In austere times it may be necessary to increase class sizes in selected areas. It may be a goal to establish part-time, evening degree programs to reach the atypical, older, married, goal-oriented student population. Again, the allocation model should reward endeavors along these lines. Likewise, the institution may desire to reward department mergers with industries, and the allocation procedure could reflect positively on such innovations (under no circumstances should an allocation procedure stifle creativity, innovation or academic freedom). Such decisions, once made and clearly stated, should be reflected in the allocation model.

It is crucial that institutional goals and policy decisions as reflected in the long-range plan be known or established prior to developing and using an allocation model. Allocation models cannot and do not make decisions. Allocation models provide a concise, efficient and understandable method of allocating resources only after basic goals and policy decisions are established. Gaining knowledge, insight and commitment regarding institutional goals is often the most difficult phase of allocation model development; and as a result, the development of the long-range plan as reflected previously becomes critical.

A successful resource allocation model must be clear, reflecting planned uses of resources. If faculty members are expected to teach, do research and counsel students, then these factors should appear and be used in the allocation model that generates faculty positions. If faculty are to be encouraged to teach evenings and weekends, and/or to generate income for the division of continuing education, then different factors become important. If a certain category of funding is for expendable items, then these items should be categorized into suitable groups that can be identified in the allocation model. The appropriate reflection of use is essential if the model is to be credible and accepted by those who receive the allocated resources.

Don't rely solely on historical resource allocations

An interesting but unacceptable procedure often used in developing a resource allocation model deserves some comment. In this procedure, an array of historical data points establishes a regression equation that's used to make subsequent allocations. Although regression equations can be useful in model development, the final allocation model must not be based solely on historical allocations nor on equations which, to the non-statistically oriented resource user, have no clear justification. Unfortunately, historical resource allocations sometimes reflect continuing inequities in allocations rather than a rational approach to resource allocations.

A successful resource allocation model must use general allocation factors. It is necessary to consider broad categorical needs for most resources to be allocated. Allocation models must be viewed as averaging techniques which guide the decision maker in the allocation process, and therefore, they should not be sensitive to highly specific and detailed needs. Specific and often minor requirements of the resource user are a part of special allocations which the decision maker may choose subjectively. They should not be allowed to clutter the allocation model. In reviewing an allocation model with those who use the resources, there is always the tendency to get into a discussion of detailed needs which are believed to be unique to a particular discipline. As an example, if faculty allocations are based on classroom and laboratory student credit hour production, a department chairman will often begin to identify course by course differences in required faculty time and effort. A chairman may also be concerned about the inexperience of his or her faculty, and may claim the model does not take into account the fact that inexperienced faculty must carry a lighter student credit hour load. Some of these concerns may be valid, but an allocation model that attempts to include excessive detail invariably fails for one or more of the following reasons:

- Factors included in the model normally must be predicted several months in advance, and detailed factors are usually difficult to predict.
- Detailed or minor factors are often manipulated by users, who realize that the factors impact allocated resources and tend to overemphasize these factors in their decision making.
- Including detailed or minor factors in a model usually causes all resource users to be preoccupied with discovering still additional factors which are unique in their discipline and should be included in the model.

In summary, each factor that seems to play a role in allocation needs must be weighed carefully to see if it is a significant factor of general concern to both the administrator and the users, or if it can be more effectively and properly "averaged" into existing factors.

For those who are particularly enthusiastic about using an allocation model to allocate available resources to implement a long-range plan, the tendency to include additional complexity and detail in the model can be overwhelming. Further, the resource user who always sees his or her area or discipline as unique continues to encourage recognition of isolated factors that will divert greater resources to the area. To be realistic, however, the administrative model user must include detail in an allocation model only to the extent that the particular administrative level knows how the resources are being used. It makes no sense, for example, for a legislature, board of trustees, or even the academic vice president to be concerned about the amount or type of chemicals needed in the chemistry department. The board of regents overseeing several large universities has little reason to determine and allocate variations by discipline in funding for faculty travel to professional meetings or adjunct faculty members as opposed to regular faculty members. Unless, for example, part of the institution's long-range plan is to increase part-time, evening enrollments by using part-time faculty.

In more concrete terms, a legislature providing funding for a large state university system should use an allocation model with one or two factors. The legislature would probably be interested in the total FTE (full-time equivalent) students served as the major parameter in providing funding, and might identify a few special projects which would be funded for relatively short periods of time. Because education is people intensive, the legislature might also enact monetary constraints by limiting the amount of the total allocation that could be used for employing personnel. This would prevent over-commitment to salaried personnel in future years.

The board of regents or state department of education that receives legislative funding would be concerned with more detail. Here, allocation model parameters would identify individual institutions and probably factor in FTE students, but might make funding dependent upon different factors: undergraduate and graduate levels; part-time, evening, non-traditional level; and, at the full-time, day, traditional level. The governing board might also choose to allocate available funding in broad areas such as instruction, research, libraries and physical plant maintenance. In so doing, the authority and level of control over resources at the local university level will be somewhat reduced.

At individual universities, the vice president for academic affairs (VPAA) would use a still more complex allocation model. The VPAA may choose to emphasize teaching, research and service differently among the disciplines represented in the university and may recognize differing costs in laboratory disciplines. In addition, the VPAA may wish to encourage off-campus instruction in one or two areas. The allocation model at this level should contain a significant amount of detail compared to the model used by a state legislature.

The successful resource allocation model must be developed so it can be reduced to mathematical formulation. Regardless of the resources to be allocated, both the factors controlling the allocation and the resources allocated are ultimately numerical quantities which, no matter how difficult, must be related mathematically. Any other alternative requires that the allocation be made subjectively. Although one expects the administrator to make a limited number of allocations based on subjective decisions (perhaps as little as 1 percent or as much as 10 percent of the total allocation), stability of the system requires that most of the allocation be made more objectively.

A mathematical formulation of a model permits both the allocator and the user to state clearly the allocation procedure. Each can predict future allocations by estimating anticipated work loads and total resources, and examining the long-range plan. It also becomes possible to assess quickly the effects of small changes in a well-established model when proposed changes are being considered. This is critical if significant change is desired in the short range.

A resource allocation model must actively involve those who will use or reallocate available resources. This involvement must center on the rationale for resource allocation and not on the quantity of the resource which any given model will produce. Little is ever accomplished in developing or modifying an allocation model if the discussion centers on the resources to be received by the user. Predictably, such discussions always result in a favorable response from those who will receive increased resources and disapproval by those who will receive less resources.

Development of a resource allocation model should be initiated by someone who knows the availability and the use of resources, and who is intimately involved in the allocation process. Factors related to the resource needs are easily identified, and it often becomes a function of the office of institutional research to gather data on how expenditures have occurred in the past. Although historical data should not control resource allocation model development, it can give clues to appropriate allocation factors, as well as to past allocation inequities, especially in light of the goals in a new long-range plan.

The following steps are normally required to establish a new allocation model:

1) Someone with budget responsibility, working with the office of institutional research and the long-range planning document, must determine significant allocation factors and parameters in the dissemination of funds.

2) Through discussion with high-level administrators, determine how policies, goals and objectives will impact budgetary policy. The long-range plan with its written goals and specific objectives will help clarify major administrative desires for budgetary emphasis.

3) Discussions with resource users and levels of administration below where the model is developed is essential to determine how the users view their needs and major resource requirements in light of the long-range plan. This group will be most impacted by the model, and their input is crucial if it's to succeed.

4) A written document outlining the allocation model must be prepared. The document must include both the rationale of the allocation procedure and the specific procedure by which the allocation will be made.

5) The written document must be reviewed and approved by administrators responsible for resource allocation.

6) The written document must be reviewed by resource users.

This last step is of prime importance in developing a satisfactory allocation model. These individuals must provide, by one means or another, the final rationale for the allocations to be made, and must have reached reasonable accord that the model will acceptably distribute the available resources for change to occur successfully. This process requires considerable time and effort, and continues as the model undergoes change and refinement each year. Resource users must participate in the LRP review process to ensure its understanding and acceptance. In addition, it's essential that users wrestle with alternatives to the model if they are to understand and appreciate the complexities of budgetary allocation.

Formula-based resource allocation models

The examples presented in the following paragraphs suggest an allocation process that might be developed in an office of academic affairs.

Example 1: The allocation of faculty positions.

The development of an allocation process requires discussion of factors which bear a direct relationship to the need for a particular resource. Once these factors are determined, each factor must be prioritized and evaluated. Naturally, disagreements will occur, and it becomes the task of higher-level administrators to review the arguments and develop acceptable compromises. Questions which might be raised in the development of an allocation process for faculty positions include the following:

- What tasks are required of typical faculty members?
- Are these tasks equally distributed and required across disciplines, or do disciplines differ significantly?
- What factors determine the need for faculty positions in each task identified?

A number of conclusions about the need for faculty positions might be reached after review and discussion by deans and department chairpersons. For example, administrators would probably conclude the major need for faculty positions is for instruction, with important additional needs in the areas of research, creative activities, student counseling, service on university committees and administrative tasks. They might also conclude that research and creative activities are important faculty activities in all academic departments, and the distribution of this research should be based on department size. Further discussion might suggest the number of positions for instruction should be based on the number of students served, recognizing that average class sizes the number of faculty needed will differ among disciplines. For example, departments that teach classes in the lecture mode will need fewer faculty positions than departments that teach most classes in a laboratory setting. The discussion might center on class sizes that would permit an acceptable level of quality in the instructional process. Of course, it must be recognized that resources are finite. Sooner or later, acceptable class sizes in each discipline have to be stated. When this is done, and when other important factors have been identified, an explicit statement of the allocation process can be made. A general description of the faculty allocation model might include the following major categories for allocating faculty positions:

- An allocation of faculty positions for instruction based on the anticipated student credit hour load in each discipline. The expected average student credit productivity per faculty member would differ depending on the discipline and whether the instruction will be at the lower, upper or graduate levels.
- An allocation of faculty positions for academic counseling. This allocation might be dependent on the number of student majors being served, or on specific discipline-dependent counseling needs. (The number of foreign or minority students who might require additional counseling could impact faculty positions for counseling.)
- An allocation of faculty positions for research, creative activities and service, including work on university committees and off-campus non-instructional activities that benefit the university.
- An allocation of faculty positions for administrative duties. Faculty positions allocated by the office of academic affairs include department chairpersons, assistant deans and graduate program coordinators.

In actual use, few of the positions identified above would be used exclusively for the purpose stated. Instead, individual faculty members might be assigned 60 percent of their time to direct instruction, 20 percent to student counseling and 20 percent to service activities. In other words, the methodology being described is intended to provide a way to calculate the total number of faculty positions allocated to the college or department. Decisions on how each position is actually assigned will be made by the college and department administrators in consultation with individual faculty members.

Using the four major categories listed above for identifying needed faculty positions, the coordinator responsible for developing the allocation model must identify factors and relationships that can be used to calculate necessary faculty positions in each category and discipline. To do so, he or she would review the long-range plan, discuss policy issues with appropriate administrators, consider available data which might provide typical average position needs and prepare a written document describing the method of calculation and rationale used. The result might appear as follows. The figures shown below approximate those used in a public university.

Allocation methodology for faculty positions

- Instructional Positions: Number equals estimated student credit hours divided by an average faculty productivity factor by student level and discipline.

Instructional faculty positions are calculated by estimating student credit hour loads and applying productivity factors for each discipline. Productivity factors are derived by specifying instructional modes (i.e. lecture, laboratory, case method, etc.) by level for every class and by identifying acceptable class sizes for every mode of instruction. Productivity factors change slightly each year due to changing patterns of course offerings. Typical productivity factors are shown in the Table 1 (see chart, next page). Student credit hours shown per position correspond to the average number of credit hours produced during the fall, spring and summer semesters by full-time faculty members.

- Counseling Positions: Number equals one full-time faculty position for every 400 student majors in the department or discipline.

Faculty positions are needed and assigned for academic counseling. This allocation is based on the equivalent of one faculty position for every 400 student majors officially enrolled in the department or discipline. In other words, it is assumed, theoretically, that a faculty member assigned solely to counseling could advise 400 student majors throughout the year.

- Faculty Activities Positions: Number equals one full-time faculty position for every 11 faculty positions allocated for instruction.

Faculty positions are needed and assigned to accomplish creative activity, research, curriculum development and public service. This allocation is made on the basis of one faculty member for every 11 faculty member allocated for instruction without regard to discipline or level of instruction. Stated differently, this allocation assumes the institution can devote slightly less than 10 percent of its faculty resources to research, creative activities and service.

- Academic Administration Positions: Number equals one full-time faculty position for every 15 faculty positions generated in instruction, counseling and faculty activities combined.

Faculty positions are needed and assigned for the purpose of providing academic administration and faculty governance. This allocation is made on the basis of one faculty position for every 15 positions generated for instruction, counseling and faculty activities, and identifies faculty positions that can be devoted to administrative tasks. In actual practice, few faculty positions will be devoted solely to academic administration. But when all partial assignments are added together, the total is expected to be approximately the number calculated in this category for the department or other budgetary unit.

The example of an allocation model for faculty positions as outlined above is one of many options that could be expected to evolve in a college or university. Important factors will depend upon the history of the institution, potential constraints imposed by the governing board, and the goals and objectives outlined in the institutional long-range plan. The model identifies the planned use of resources, and permits an immediate calculation of the number of faculty positions to be allocated once the expected student credit hour loads in each program or discipline are known. The model is easily administered using minimal computing capability, and permits estimates of future year allocations if the information is needed. Perceived inadequacies in the model are discussed during the mid-year when the pressure to allocate resources is not the primary issue. Such discussions center on improvements in the methodology of the model rather than on actual resources to be allocated or

Table 1: Example of Instructional Faculty Productivity Factors.

Annual Student Credit Hours Per Full Time Position
Employed Fall, Spring and Summer Semesters and
Assigned Solely to Instruction (By Level)

College & Discipline	Lower Level	Upper Level	Graduate Level
Arts & Sciences			
Biol Science	1397	899	594
Communications	800	1150	487
Computer Science	1507	1284	619
Fine Arts	1147	743	319
Foreign Language	1089	1067	637
Letters	920	1136	657
Math & Statistics	1120	1120	605
Physical Science	1298	886	440
Psychology	3712	1364	522
Public Affairs	1740	1397	789
Social Science	3020	1422	613
BUSINESS ADMINISTRATION	1392	1408	641
EDUCATION	1392	1218	732
ENGINEERING	1557	1028	536
HEALTH	1086	701	616

received. Finally, the procedure is consistent from year to year, since changes in the model are gradual and have limited impact over the short term.

Allocating operating expenses

Factors that determine the need for operating expense funds can often be identified using expenditure data from prior years. Discussions and decisions by administrators should center on the identification of broad categories of needs requiring funding, and whether or not such funding is needed across disciplines. Broad categories might include instructional supplies, travel costs, communications (telephone, postage) and the cost of service contracts on equipment.

An example of an operating expense allocation model is described below. Note that most categories are broad, and make use of highly aggregated average costs in setting the allocation parameters. This model is used by the office of academic affairs in major universities.

The expense categories described below refer to the allocation of operating expense needed in academic colleges and departments. Other categories would be needed to describe operating expense requirements in areas such as general administration, the registrar's office and student affairs.

- Instructional Operating Costs: Funding equals $600 per FTE faculty position.

This category includes the costs of telephone service, paper, pencils, xeroxing, and other general needs in college and departmental offices.

- Professional Travel: Funding equals $750 per FTE faculty position.

This category includes funds used to offset all or part of faculty travel costs to professional meetings. The amount allocated per faculty member is intended to be an average expenditure. The amount available to individual faculty members will depend on policies established in the colleges and departments.

- Instructional Travel and Meals: Funding equals $7 per off-campus student credit hour.

These funds are used to pay the cost of travel and meals for faculty who teach courses away from the main campus. The calculation provides an average funding level for off-campus instructional activity. It is based on historical experience and the projected off-campus effort in the year for which the allocation is made.

- Discipline Dependent Workload: Funding equals $5 per weighted student credit hour. These funds are utilized to purchase class related expendable supplies, and to repair and maintain existing equipment. The workload weighting factors are shown in Table 2. The factors reflect significant differences in the need for expendable supplies among disciplines, departments and colleges.

The operating expense allocation model described above is one of many which might evolve following discussions with academic deans and department chairs. Noticeably missing from the listing of expense categories (if costs are charged back to departments) is the cost of mainframe computing. Note that each category used in the allocation model reflects an actual use of operating expense funds. This procedure gives the model credibility with both administrators and faculty.

The discipline dependent workload category is the most difficult to establish, and one that often requires judgmental decisions. This is also the category that's likely to change most rapidly. The workload weighting factors are multiplied by the total student credit hour production anticipated in each discipline to obtain weighted student credit hours. In this model, the disciplines of foreign language and public affairs are considered to have minimal needs for class-related expendable supplies. Biological sciences, on the other hand, is known to need laboratory supplies and chemicals, all of which must be replaced each year. In addition, the department of biological sciences has many items of equipment requiring maintenance and repairs.

The workload weighting factor in business administration is an example of one that's changed significantly in recent years. This discipline has placed heavy emphasis on computing, and now must purchase software and maintain computing equipment for use by faculty and students.

The operating expense model is structured to permit calculations using a personal computer. Input data consists of student hour estimates and the number of faculty positions in each discipline. If the faculty allocation model described previously has been used to calculate the number of faculty positions, the operating expense calculation can be programmed to run automatically from the faculty allocation model.

Table 2: Examples of Workload Weighting Factors

Workload Weighting Factors

Discipline	Student Credit Hours Weighting Factor
ARTS & SCIENCES	
Biol Science	1.00
Communications	0.40
Computer Science	0.70
Fine Arts	0.75
Foreign Language	0.01
Letters	0.05
Math & Statistics	0.10
Physical Science	0.90
Psychology	0.50
Public Affairs	0.01
Social Science	0.05
BUSINESS ADMINISTRATION	0.20
EDUCATION	0.20
ENGINEERING	0.70
HEALTH	0.70

Allocating faculty salaries

Allocating faculty salary funding is a sensitive issue, and one that's usually highly constrained. In colleges and universities, salary dollar constraints may be imposed by the board of trustees, the legislature, board of regents, a faculty union and state statutes. In addition, campus administrators must recognize cost-of-living increases, merit and marketplace conditions. The formulation of a rigorous and quantitative procedure may be difficult, but systematic procedures can be identified, and are described in the following paragraphs.

At least three factors are important in allocating faculty salary resources:

- College deans and department chairs must have some flexibility to recognize outstanding faculty performance through merit salary increases.
- The retention of top faculty members is essential for the continued strength and academic growth of the institution, and requires the payment of nationally competitive salaries.
- The recruitment of quality faculty is essential to the strength and academic growth of the institution and requires competitive new-hire salaries.

Faculty salaries are highly dependent on discipline. It's no longer unusual to find average salaries in some disciplines that are twice the average salaries in other disciplines. The same can be said of average new hire salaries. These differences need to be recognized in the salary allocation policy.

The policy for allocating salary funding is often further complicated by the existing status of faculty salaries. Because salary administration is difficult and sensitive, salary increases tend to be equalized each year across disciplines. As a result, disciplines that are experiencing significant average salary increases in the national marketplace often lag behind locally, while those that are static nationally have a relative advantage. It is not surprising that disciplines locally that lag behind national salary averages are also the ones in which faculty members are in demand and mobile. Such institutions are clearly in danger of losing the best faculty in these disciplines and may be unable to compete for quality replacements.

If the institution is to maintain a competitive position, particularly in disciplines with high student demand and high average salaries nationally, the salary administration policy must reflect the national marketplace, making differential discipline salary increases mandatory. Administrators must find ways to minimize the disruptive aspects of a differential salary increase policy by making the rationale for the policy and the data supporting it widely known and understood.

A faculty salary allocation procedure that recognizes discipline differences and variations in the national marketplace is described in the following paragraphs:

1) Current faculty salary status at the institution: Existing institutional faculty salaries will be a matter of record, and should be summarized in a table showing discipline and rank information. The second column in Table 3 (see chart) provides an abbreviated and hypothetical example of the needed data.

2) Comparison of existing faculty salaries to national or regional data for comparable institutions: National data is available from several sources, such as the American Association of University Professors (AAUP), the American Association of State Colleges and Universities (AASCU) and the Oklahoma State

Table 3: Comparison of Institutional and National Salary Data (Example)

Discipline	Number of Faculty	Institutional Salary Total Level	National Average Salary Level Salary (Total)	Percent Above (Below) National Average
Discipline A				
Instructor	2	$38,000	$39,824	(4.58)
Assistant Professor	6	$154,812	$163,806	(5.49)
Associate Professor	5	$143,210	$162,855	(12.06)
Professor	4	$141,016	$150,200	(6.11)
Total		$477,038	$516,658	(7.67)
Discipline B				
Instructor	6	$21,320	$21,000	(1.52)
Assistant Professor	5	$167,830	$160,995	(4.25)
Associate Professor	6	$225,072	$222,526	(1.14)
Professor	4	$210,192	$207,360	(1.37)
Total		$624,414	$611,881	(2.05)
Discipline C				
Instructor	3	$54,714	$52,000	(5.22)
Assistant Professor	8	$198,264	$194,720	(1.82)
Associate Professor	10	$271,200	$280,290	(3.24)
Professor	12	$493,056	$537,744	(8.31)
Total		$1,017,234	$1,064,754	(4.46)
Institutional Total		$2,118,686	$2,193,320	(3.40)

University Faculty Salary Survey. Alternatively, an independent study of comparable institutions can provide the needed data. This information is utilized to provide comparisons with existing institutional salaries. The third column in Table 3 summarizes the comparative data for this example.

3) The allocation of salary dollars: As the data in Table 3 shows, Discipline B is in the best position relative to the national marketplace. Assuming there are no specific administrative reasons for this variation, available salary increase funding should be distributed to correct or partially correct the observed differences compared to the marketplace. A procedure for making the needed adjustment follows, with the assumption that an average salary increase of 5 percent is available.

- **Across-the-board or cost-of-living increase:** Allocating part of the available salary increase dollars uniformly to faculty in each discipline may be required by faculty union negotiations or viewed as appropriate by institutional administrators. In this example, it's assumed that approximately one half (2.5 percent of the current salary base) of the available increase in salary funding will be allocated for across the board or cost of living increases. The calculation is shown in Table 3 under the heading Salary Increase Funding — Fixed.

- **Merit salary increase:** Institutional administrators need to have flexibility to reward meritorious service and the achievement of the objectives outlined in the long-range plan. For purposes of this example, it is assumed that 2 percent of the base salary total in each discipline will be used for merit increases. The calculation is shown in Table 4.

TABLE 4: Distribution of Salary Increase Funding (Example)

Discipline	Salary Total	Salary Increase Funding Fixed 2.5 %	Merit 2%	Marketplace 2%	Percent Increase Total
Discipline A	$ 47,038	11,926	9,541	5,507	5.65
Discipline B	624,414	15,610	12,488	0	4.50
Discipline C	1,017,234	25,431	20,345	5,086	5.00
Total	$ 2,118,686	52,967	42,374	10,593	5.00

- Marketplace salary adjustment: Table 3 provides the basis for allocating the remaining one-half percent of the base salary total in all disciplines if marketplace competitiveness is viewed as an institutional priority. One alternative would be to allocate none of the marketplace adjustment to Discipline B and distribute the funds instead to Disciplines A and C. The distribution to Disciplines A and C should be based on the relative differences between the institutional salaries paid in these disciplines and those paid in the marketplace. Table 4 shows the approximate result of this alternative but retains the 5 percent average increase in Discipline C.

The salary allocation described in this limited example will move Discipline A to a slightly more competitive position in the national marketplace, adjusts Discipline B to a slightly less competitive position and holds Discipline C at the same competitive level, relative to current national average salaries. The trade-off represents one of many difficult decisions that beset the budget allocation process. Table 5 summarizes

Discipline	Percent Above (Below) the National Marketplace Before Salary Increases	Percent Above (Below) the National Marketplace After Salary Increases
Discipline A	(7.67)	(7.01)
Discipline B	2.05	1.56
Discipline C	(4.46)	(4.46)

TABLE 5: Changes in Relative Marketplace Position (Example)

the changes in relative marketplace position that would occur using this example. The change is small, but if the procedure is used consistently each year, the goal of maintaining competitiveness in the national marketplace among different disciplines will be achieved.

❑❑❑

Of all of Deming's points, this is the one we found most frequently violated when we presented workshops for academic institutions. Most colleges and universities lack a constancy of purpose; i.e. their mission statements were so broad as to be useless. The institution was to be all things to all people. Furthermore, when a long-range plan existed, it sat on the shelf gathering dust, since the resource allocation procedure was not tied to the implementation of the plan. In other words, after the planning was done, it was business as usual, since very few people knew the institution's mission. And if they did, there was funding sufficient to implement about 75 percent of the activities. Of course, there were institutions whose employees not only knew the mission statement, but also tied meaningful long-range planning to resource allocation. These institutions, such as William Rainey Harper College in Palatine, IL, encourage innovation and quality.

In workshops we've presented, administrators have cited the following factors as inhibiting quality at their institutions:

- Inadequate funding.
- Poor student preparation.
- Aging faculty.
- Poor teaching.
- Poor faculty morale.
- Collective bargaining.
- Inadequate facilities.
- Faculty resistance to change.

The root of these problems is poor planning and resource allocation, both of which are controlled by administration.

In the School of Science, Management & Technologies (SM&T) at Edinboro University of Pennsylvania (EUP), we have involved the faculty and chairpersons in creating a constancy of purpose toward improvement. Using the aforementioned techniques, each department has determined its strengths and weaknesses, and established its priorities based on this information. The plan has been used to produce a resource allocation formula, which in turn, drives the plan. The net effect is that resources are available to implement top priorities. The consequent reduction in uncertainty and arbitrariness has had an immediate positive effect on morale, productivity and commitment among department personnel.

Table 6 shows an example of a resource allocation formula for equipment dollars used by various SM&T departments. Although there is never enough money to purchase all of the required equipment, the allocation of the money that became available was done on the basis of the department's equipment intensity and the number of students the department served, i.e. the number of student credit hours generated.

Table 6: Formula used to allocate equipment money at SM&T

Academic Department	Av. 3 yr SCH	Weighting Factor*	Weighted SCH**	Percent Allocation	Amount
Biol & Hlth Svs	8871	0.17	1508.07	26.41	$14811.92
Business & Econ	12945	0.05	647.25	11.34	$6357.14
Chemistry	3049	0.17	518.33	9.08	$5090.92
Geosciences			0.00	0.00	$0.00
Geology	4885	0.17	830.45	14.54	$8156.49
Geography	7069	0.02	141.38	2.48	$1388.60
Math & Computer Sci.			0.00	0.00	$0.00
Math	10769	0.02	215.38	3.77	$2115.41
Computer Science	6512	0.12	781.44	13.69	$7675.13
Nursing	2584	0.15	387.60	6.79	$3806.92
Physics & Tech	3998	0.17	679.66	11.90	$6675.47
TOTAL	60682		5709.56	100	$56078.00

* Note: The weighting factor ranged from 0 to 0.2.
**Note: Weighted SCH equals the average 3 year SCH x Weighting Factor

Chapter 2:
Adopt the new philosophy

"The act of courage is to say what needs to be said to those that need to hear it. Being authentic is putting into words what we see happening. An important part of being authentic is expressing the first two elements of courage: the harsh reality facing us and our own contributions to the problem. Often people feel that to be authentic in this way is to be suicidal. They claim other people don't want to hear bad news (the harsh reality) and why add insult to injury by announcing that there is not only bad news, but they are partly to blame for it. This fear of others' disapproval starts the whole bureaucratic cycle. ... Being authentic even in the face of disapproval is at any time the unique contribution we have to make. It does go against culture, because most cultures are engaged in role playing, looking good, disguising problems — all variations on running for office. Being authentic is a risk worth taking and does require courage" (Block, p. 187).

There must be a new way of thinking in higher education about how to ensure continuing improvement in processes and people. This is more than solving problems. Since we are dealing with immense questions, it is not enough to know a lot of little answers. A new philosophy for adopting quality must infiltrate the entire institution. We can't have a first class society with second class colleges and universities.

Tom Peters, in his book <u>Thriving on Chaos</u> (1987, p. 560), states: *"To up the odds of survival, leaders at all levels must become obsessive about change. They must: In the matter of formal and informal evaluations of leaders (managers at all levels), focus less on measures that deal with such things as budgets, and more on the explicit questions: 'What exactly have you changed lately?' Additionally, every meeting should commence with a rapid, explicit review of exactly what has been changed since the last session, even if it was yesterday; every newsletter should emphasize change; and so on."*

Change is a potent factor in higher education. People fear it, resent it and ignore it, but it's inevitable. We must ask, therefore, in what direction the change will take place, how rapidly the change will occur and how change can be directed so higher education can take advantage of it. Change is constant. What is frightening about it is that the rate of change forms an exponential curve, and by standing still, higher education loses ground. Thus, if higher education is to have a meaningful mission we must plan well to meet change. This requires vision tempered with probability; the agenda of the possible. Accommodating change requires a continuing commitment to terminate obsolete methods and programs, as well as to develop new ones. We will not be content to rest on laurels or to stagnate at the status quo if we honestly execute our responsibilities.

Changes must be consistent with the mission of higher education. All persons affected by change must plan for it and believe in the value of the proposed change and in their ability to carry it out. Success is enhanced if success is expected.

We can no longer live with ineffective but commonly accepted styles, nor with accepted levels of mistakes, delays and uneducated graduates. Such management brings about waste of manpower and other resources. No one should have to subsidize this waste.

The American people should not have to tolerate an uneducated graduate. Graduates should be able to read, write, speak, perform mathematical functions, be computer literate, think critically, have a sense of values, etc. A graduate of one of the professional disciplines should, in addition to liberal education competencies, have skills necessary for employment. Everyone *must* adopt this philosophy.

We are in a new economic age of a worldwide marketplace — no longer can America dominate world affairs through mediocre efforts. One of the key ingredients in the new worldwide competition is the quality of higher education. People associated with higher education should not tolerate careless mistakes, unsuitable materials, damaged equipment, inadequate training, ineffective supervision or vague directions and expectations

Quehl (1988, p. 37) stated: *"As a nation struggles with trade deficits and finds it difficult to compete in business with other countries worldwide, many people look to colleges and universities to help solve this problem."* Most universities don't teach statistical quality control measures, values and morals with respect to the long-term gain for society. We lack these competencies not only in our business, law and medical curriculums, but in most of our professional programs. If higher education adds these items to curriculums and if we expect students to master them before they graduate, our nation might address international trade more effectively after 20 or more years.

According to Lodge (1988, p. 35), *"learning means understanding that most of the problems of our high-tech industries derive from America's traditional ideology of individualism, from the very hymns that we as a nation love to sing."* Yet, very few, if any, major universities teach the importance of cooperation; of win-win negotiations, rather than the typical winner take all attitude. No one — students, faculty or administrators — are rewarded for cooperation. He further states: *"According to this ideology, the legitimacy of business derives from the notion of property rights, and the authority of its managers derives from its owners, the shareholders. The managers' primary purpose is satisfaction of those shareholders. To this end managers compete to satisfy consumer demand in a marketplace rigorously kept open by antitrust laws."*

Quehl (1988) had similar observations regarding higher education in his interviews: *"While the nation needs a citizenry not only skilled at vocations but also schooled in morals, values, history, ideas, choices, civics and other citizen-based attributes, both college students and their parents ... are crassly materialistic in what they expect a college education to provide (p. 37)... If international economic competition is an omnibus issue facing the nation as a whole, then economic competition among the states clearly guides the agendas in most state capitals"* (p. 39). These are a direct result of living in a fish-eyed, instant gratification society. While our competitors enjoy a good working relationship among their government, industries and educational institutions, we have permitted a ... *"deterioration of our educational system and the erosion of our skill base"* (Lodge 1988, p. 36). Many of our international economic problems are a direct result of living in an individualistic, instant gratification society — by the same token, these are the values we continue to teach in colleges and universities. Higher education must respond by revising the terminal competencies we expect from our graduates to serve society better.

Adopting the new quality philosophy means eliminating repeated, careless mistakes that indicate either something is wrong with the system or that individuals have been assigned to jobs they aren't prepared for. Either the system requires change or the individual requires training or reassignment to a job to which he or she is better suited. In any case, repeated mistakes are not to be "brushed off." That sends a clear message that carelessness is tolerated.

Poor policies, antiquated equipment, vague directions and poor professional development plans, for example, will result in the faculty and staff not being allowed or able to perform their responsibilities at a level necessary to produce desired results.

Students should not have to tolerate poorly qualified professors. By the same token, professors should not have to tolerate inadequate teaching facilities, antiquated equipment, poorly prepared students and an ineffective administration. Administration should constantly improve in locating the necessary funding not only to improve the facilities, equipment and the assessment of students, but to improve the professional development of faculty and staff.

Unsuitable materials and damaged equipment rob employees of their right to do a good job. Situations involving unsuitable materials and damaged equipment can occur anywhere in an institution: support offices, classrooms and student support areas. Tolerating damaged equipment sends a negative message to staff and students that equipment isn't valuable.

Vague directions and expectations should not be tolerated. To perform well, people should have clear directions and an understanding of expectations. For the institutional staff, a clear plan helps to minimize the need for specific directions. But when directions are given, they must be clear. A person who is consistently given vague directions will become frustrated and will ultimately refuse to accept responsibility. Students also have a right to be provided with clear directions and a well-defined set of expectations for campus life and classroom performance.

Every student should be required to take a comprehensive freshman orientation course, or at least have a comprehensive orientation to the "society" of campus life. In campus life, student behavior deteriorates if the "rules of campus living" are not well defined.

In the classroom, performance suffers when students get obscure directions, and when they don't know what's expected of them. Faculty, therefore, should produce course syllabi that include the expected terminal competencies, objectives, reading list, and method(s) of assessment, as well as policies and other pertinent course information. Every student should have such a syllabus for each course.

As in industry, the impact of foreign competition is being felt in American higher education. Here also, a future-oriented strategy, based on a philosophy of continuing improvement, can enhance quality and productivity by directing analysis and action toward correcting the process itself.

Although the goal of producing educated graduates never changes, ways to arrive at that goal must constantly improve. All personnel must be allowed to be responsible for their own duties. In many cases, higher education personnel are given responsibilities but are hindered in fulfilling them by undue interference from the next level. This is usually the direct result of poor policies. Because most evaluation systems reward individuals on recognition rather than cooperation, people try to please the "boss" rather than improve the system by pointing out mistakes (see Points 8 and 12).

A university needs an operational philosophy that makes the best use of all talents to produce higher quality graduates in a more efficient way. Few people come to a job perfectly prepared for the demands that will be placed on them. It is essential that the institution have ongoing training programs for each position within the institution. Training programs need not be extensive or formal, but should, at a minimum, define the responsibilities of the position and make special training available when warranted. All staff members need to have their skills maintained or upgraded, and must be reminded of the basic philosophy of constant improvement guiding the institution. Effective training can be the end product of successful mentoring. We recommend mentoring for all faculty and staff (in fact, as we mention later, we recommend a comprehensive mentoring program for the entire university/college community).

Training and experiences involving all people in moving toward effective teaching or other service must be provided. In-service training should not only include the mechanics of doing the job, but also personal growing experiences. Barriers that prevent faculty and staff from exercising alternatives must be removed. Helping faculty and staff to grow and improve professionally and personally will return great dividends. Effective professional service is a byproduct of a deep commitment.

Supervision implies the organizing of personnel and resources to carry out an assigned set of tasks. The supervisor must create or maintain the necessary organization so assigned tasks are carried out efficiently. If the institution adopts Deming's philosophy, each supervisor must thoroughly understand this philosophy, communicate it to the staff and then apply it. A unit within the institution that shows consistent disorganization, unresponsiveness, lack of creativity or low morale is a unit lacking proper supervision.

Figure 1: Process for Change

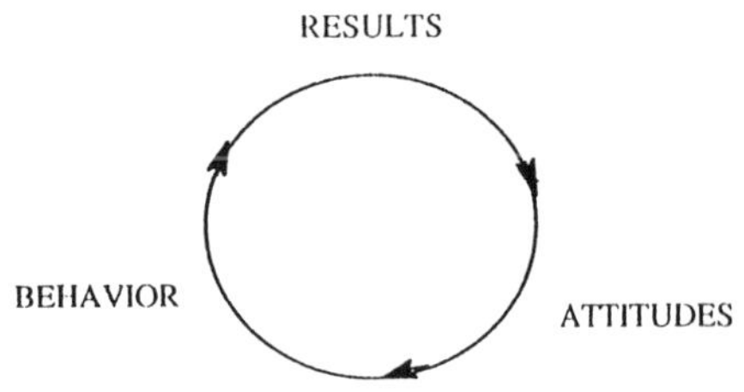

RESULTS

BEHAVIOR

ATTITUDES

Most institutions are in a pattern where established attitudes give rise to a given behavior, yielding particular results. If there is a goal to establish better quality, people must be motivated to change. The process that is in place in most institutions is depicted in Figure 1. Faculty and administrators have set attitudes that guide their behavior and yield a particular set of results, which may be either good or bad. The systems and processes are cumbersome, and as a result, there is little opportunity to demonstrate pride in workmanship. To report failures or to suggest improvements in the systems or processes would cause great apprehension, and therefore, people are not motivated to improve constantly. The cycle is self-perpetuating: a standard

34

set of attitudes yields a standard set of behaviors, which yield a standard set of results.

A process for change

In one university we became aware of difficulties in producing a schedule of classes that was not riddled with errors. The schedules were first manually entered on a form by the department chairperson. The chairperson forwarded the schedule to the dean, who either made changes in the schedule after consultation with the chairperson, or forwarded the schedule to the registrar. The registrar gave the schedules to either work study students or to secretaries who had to enter the data into the main frame computer. The computer center generated the schedules (and the work load of the faculty). The registrar forwarded the computer-generated schedules back to the dean and department chairpersons. They were asked to check the schedules and the workloads of the faculty. Because of the incorrect entries by the "workers on the line" (secretaries and work study students), many errors were found, including: (1) an art faculty member was assigned to a course in history; (2) a deceased faculty member was scheduled for three courses in rooms that were to be used by another department; (3) sections were either added, deleted or scheduled at times inappropriate for the particular course, and (4) some faculty members were being credited for 60 work hours (24 work hours was the normal load for this institution) while others were scheduled for as little as four work hours. After the errors were corrected by the chairpersons and the dean, the cycle continued for two or three additional checks! Then after the final check, the schedule was sent to the printers. After returning from the printers, the schedules had so many mistakes that 10,000 copies had to be destroyed and another "rush" job, for which the university paid dearly, had to be done. Then, two pages of corrections had to be included. As shown in Figure 1, certain results (poor schedules) yielded certain attitudes (frustration) which yielded certain behaviors (accusations of incompetence).

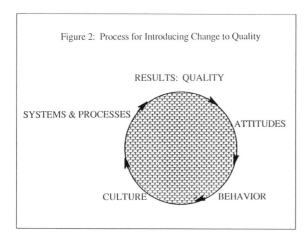

Figure 2: Process for Introducing Change to Quality

RESULTS: QUALITY

SYSTEMS & PROCESSES

ATTITUDES

CULTURE

BEHAVIOR

But if a commitment to quality is made with the simultaneous introduction of new systems and processes, the results will reflect better quality. Better quality brings more pride in workmanship, resulting in a change of attitudes and behaviors. In fact, the behavior can become a "culture" within the company (such as Team Taurus in Ford Motor Company). Culture can be defined as the issues of the institution that are related to the assumptions and values that will determine how people will perform within the college or university. Such a culture will insist on better systems and processes, which will give better results — the cycle will result in constant improvement (see Figure 2).

Introducing change toward quality

In the university where the course scheduling fiasco was mentioned, the registrar suggested that since the entire campus was tied into the main frame computer, the department chairs and dean should enter an error free schedule directly onto the main frame. Then the schedule would be delivered to the printers within one week, rather than the six-month turnaround time required by the check, check, and re-check process. The system was improved, which resulted in quality results (an error-free schedule) supporting a positive attitude (a job well done), which resulted in a change of behavior (teaming) and a culture (that we do it right the first time).

All institutions have priorities, although the system of guiding the priorities may be invisible. Clear priorities can make the difference between a mediocre and a high-quality operation. Basic to clarifying priorities is the reason that every individual must have an opportunity to help determine the priorities and structure of the institution. Communication is extremely important in higher education. People need to know who and/or what controls the content and flow of information. The truth must be told.

An institution of higher education has a responsibility to its service area and its immediate community to cooperate on programs that meet people' s needs. Also, no educational institution, public or private, can attain its highest potential without taking advantage of all external sources of support. Such resources and the possibilities that can result will carry an institution beyond its mission.

In adopting the new philosophy management must realize that it does not mean that the faculty and staff will run the institution. In fact, a close analysis of Deming's philosophy will show that Deming promotes an elite management, i.e. one capable of taking good data and advice from the entire population they serve and support to make good decisions in a timely fashion to increase quality and public acceptance. Even when one examines the Japanese industries that use this management style, such as Toyota, one finds that the final decisions are made by a small group of managers. By the same token, the managers implement over 95 percent of the more than 10,000 yearly suggestions supplied by the work force. This is important because many presidents, vice presidents and deans feel threatened by terms such as "empowering" employees. On the other hand, some institutions, such as William Rainey Harper College, under the strong leadership of the president and administration, are instituting the Deming process to ensure quality, public acceptance and positioning. As demographics change in the coming years, one can only ask which institutions will survive and capture market share and public funding.

"Fishbone" charts encourage quality

In the School of Science, Management & Technologies (SM&T) at Edinboro University of Pennsylvania, we instituted a series of management systems as a result of the long-range plan and resource allocation procedure. The systems approach included such things as management by policy deployment and "fishbone" charts that encouraged faculty and staff to suggest ways to increase efficiency and quality. The results of the "fishbone" charts were published in the school's newsletter, and progress has been made in resolving several of the issues that inhibited quality instruction and performance in SM&T.

These approaches resulted in a more vocal faculty and staff and complemented the strong emphasis on change and innovation. As a result, an obvious increase in "risk factors" was noted among the faculty and staff as they tried new things in an effort to improve quality. Some examples are noted below.

Several secretaries, trained to think in the Deming's system approach, were able to modify several forms and routine office procedures that were, at best, cumbersome.

The chairperson of mathematics and computer science noted that on the average three students dropped out of the freshman course in computer science, a course that was required for general education. Since 12 or more sections of the course were offered every semester, 36 seats went unfilled. He began to call those students that did not show up for the first several classes and told them they were out of the class. He then filled these seats with students from a waiting list he compiled.

We mentioned previously that we used fishbone charts to determine perceived causes to problems (see Figure 3 for a sample fishbone chart). We would post these charts throughout high traffic areas for groups we were trying to reach. A typical fishbone chart citing a perceived problem (negative attitudes toward students) was placed in the dean's office so students could give their perceptions as to the causes.

Figure 3

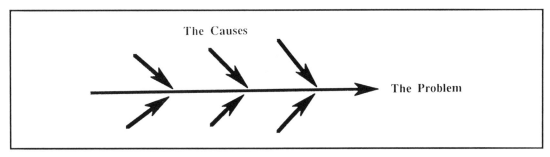

This resulted in a serious effort of faculty, staff and administration to be much more sensitive to the needs of the customer.

Fishbone charts identifying poor ratings of professors by students as a problem were placed throughout several departmental offices. The responses by faculty resulted in a suggested total revision of the faculty evaluation procedure.

Before the Deming philosophy was adopted, chairpersons at SM&T inferred that the main problems with increasing faculty performance and morale were due to:
- Management-union antagonism (60 percent).
- Incompetent and vindictive administration (40 percent).

The perceived strengths of the institution were:
- Committed faculty.
- Solid academic programs.

After preparing and instituting the long-range plan and resource allocation procedure, and adopting Deming's quality philosophy, SM&T chairpersons, when subjected to a nominal group process, perceived the following to inhibit quality in the school:
- Lack of facilities (11.2 percent).
- Timeliness of administrative decisions (8 percent).
- Poor student profiles (7.6 percent).
- Micro-management by administration (7.4 percent).

- Uncommitted faculty (6.3 percent).

Interestingly, the management-union relationship was ranked 10th, receiving only 4.6 percent of the score. In addition, one of the main perceived institutional strengths in the prior year — committed faculty — was now perceived to be a major weakness.

It should be noted that the SM&T chairpersons, after adopting the quality philosophy, published and informed the administration that the management systems were getting in the way of progress in spite of previous perceptions, which were untrue, that the administration was vindictive! The chairpersons, which are part of the bargaining unit, also began to inform the union leadership of unprofessional activities of not only certain faculty, but of the executive members of the board as well.

After two years of refining and instituting the long-range plan and the Deming philosophy on quality, the SM&T chairpersons, when subjected to a nominal group process, perceived the following to inhibit quality in the school:

- Inefficient management systems (28 percent).
- Funds for classrooms and offices (22 percent).
- Stable base of resources (21 percent).
- Inability to attract quality faculty (10 percent).

At the end of two years the "we vs. them" (union and administration) feeling was not perceived as the problem. The problem, as perceived by the SM&T chairpersons, was not with the people, either union or management, but with the processes and systems at both levels. All of the chairpersons believed everyone wanted to do a good job, but they knew that management controlled at least 85 percent of the processes and systems, and was at fault. In addition, the SM&T chairpersons also knew the faculty and staff were not informing the administration on what needed to be fixed! (After all, who wants to be the bearer of bad news?)

Adopting the quality philosophy means that when something is wrong people must admit it before progress can be made to improve the process and system. It should be noted that the perceived "solid academic programs" strength of just two years prior resulted in each and every program being either substantially or totally revised after each chairperson and the faculty admitted the programs required revisions.

As a result of this new openness, several faculty began to experiment with different teaching methods, such as teleclasses, videocourses, team projects, case studies, inquiry methods and discussion, rather than using the typical lecture method. Several of the experiments resulted in presentations at an academic festival and provided ideas for future research. Faculty became interested in and attended seminars on teaching-learning styles and syllabus preparation.

SM&T secretaries also participated in quality workshops both on- and off-campus. The on-campus workshops were initially conducted by the dean of SM&T. Off-campus workshops and seminars were identified by secretaries themselves and were funded out of the office of the dean. The workshops and seminars usually lasted for the entire day. In addition, many audio and videotaped programs were purchased to help the secretaries develop their skills.

As a result of the secretaries being trained in the systems approach to quality, a nominal group process conducted after the first year identified the following problems:

- Lack of job training
- Communication within and between departments.
- Negative attitudes.
- Lack of collegiality.
- Inability to effect change.

Fishbone charts identifying lack of job training as the problem were posted in several areas. The following causes were typically noted by the secretaries:

- No orientation.
- Inaccurate job description.
- No input from faculty as to expectations.
- No office procedure training.
- No encouragement by administration.
- Lack of combined workshops on teaming for faculty, secretaries and administration.

Since the previous problems were identified, we've begun to address every issue in a timely manner. Several secretaries have mentioned they now have pride in their work since they are trusted and empowered to act on items that in the past were considered off-limits.

Chapter 3:
Cease dependence on inspection

The main product of a university is the educated graduate. Although we don't believe that testing students should be eliminated, we agree with Deming (1986, p. 28) that testing to improve quality is too late. We believe the quality of graduates will increase from improvements in selecting, advising, counseling, mentoring and assessing students — all of which are more valuable in assuring quality than routine testing procedures. In addition, matching the teaching styles of professors with the learning styles of new students is very important in the retention of students (Claxton and Murrell 1987, p. 62).

No one can doubt the importance of selecting students. A student with high SAT/ACT scores who is in the top 10 percent of a good high school graduating class will most likely do well in a university. The function of public universities, however, is to deliver a good education to a maximum number of people at the lowest possible cost. Therefore, the selection criteria should not be so discriminating as to deny the opportunity of a higher education to the masses. SAT/ACT scores should be eliminated from the selection criteria because many believe they're culturally biased and the results can be influenced by taking "crash" courses. High school grades, letters of reference, essays and personal interviews should be substituted for SAT and ACT results.

Several major problems contribute to the selection process. For example, many people don't know the difference between two- and four-year institutions and graduate and professional schools (Quehl 1988, p. 35). How can they help their children prepare for college? By the year 2000, minorities will represent nearly one-third of the college-age population (Mingle 1987, p. 1). Higher education has not been able to respond by providing social support systems to ensure a reasonable chance for graduation. Nearly one-third of the students who enter into ninth grade will not graduate from high school (The Chronicle of Higher Education, March 18, 1987, p. A26), probably because the educational system is not designed to accommodate them.

Institutions of higher education must face up to the fact that the number of illiterates graduating from high school is increasing. In 1960, the average grade for the high school student was "C" and the graduate could read at the 10th grade level. In 1989 the average grade of a high school graduate was "B" and the average reading level was at the 7-8th grade. If the results continue along the same trend, and there is every reason to believe they will during the 1990s, higher education will be receiving more, not less qualified students from our high schools. If we are going to eliminate the need for inspection on a mass basis by building quality into the product (entering freshman) in the first place, higher education and society will have to cooperate on an expansive scale. If our goal is to have students succeed, we must provide K-12 students with massive support systems and well-defined structures. We recommend that an intensive mentoring system be implemented.

Mentoring of elementary school students could be done by good high school and college students. Reports of successful mentoring of elementary and middle school students interested in science, mathematics and engineering through a college student mentoring program was reported by Jean Roberts and Pamela Freyd from the University of Pennsylvania (Diversity in Mentoring Conference Report, May 17-19, 1990, Troy, Mich.). Excellent results from mentoring high school students and beginning college students have been reported from using not only college faculty, but also staff, secretaries, retirees, peers, alumni and representatives from businesses (Diversity in Mentoring Conference Reports, May 17-19, 1990, Troy, Mich.).

In addition to mentoring, we believe four-year institutions of higher education should require all entering students to take a two-week orientation seminar prior to being admitted into classes. The orientation would involve intensive testing in basic knowledge (reading, writing, math, etc.) and learning style. Based on the results of these tests the students would be assigned only to those courses for which a reasonable chance for success is apparent. Students would also be provided information on "how to succeed" and in "stress management," and would be assigned to and meet with their mentor and advisor.

The single best predictor of success in college is class attendance, not SATs, family income or high school GPA. A college in San Marcos, CA doubled its sophomore enrollment by having faculty call students who did not show up for class. It appears that calling students who are absent may be worth trying, if not by the professor at least by the mentor.

In addition to class attendance, students who sit in the front rows have a better chance to pass than those who sit in the back. Perhaps all students who are at risk should be assigned front row seats.

Most faculty are still teaching and grading in the same manner as was done in the 1930s: they lecture and give standardized exams suitable only for students who either respond well to the lecture format or conform to this style and can regurgitate the information on such exams. Poor faculty, like fools with no talent, have the ability to turn students off. It takes faculty with talent to turn students on. Students who respond well to the typical lecture and multiple choice examination formats will most likely do well in such tests as the SAT and ACT, and their GPA will most likely reflect such conformity. The truth of the matter is that this style is not, and was never, suitable for many minority students. Yet as we enter the information era, colleges and universities are too slow in responding to the need to educate all members of society. Since it's higher education's duty to educate the population for the social welfare of our nation, our administrators encourage traditional selection and teaching processes, while professors are afraid to "fail" i.e., innovate with different teaching and assessing methods. As a result we end up humiliating many students by labeling them as "failures" when, in fact, the educational system is a failure. Unless we respond to the educational needs of the minority population, much of the population may be unemployable and thus a burden to the rest of society (Quehl 1988, p. 37).

States are attempting to ensure educational quality in three general ways: increasing admission standards, sponsoring remedial work for under-prepared college students and developing measuring techniques, including testing student knowledge and institutional performance (Quehl 1988, p. 39).

Increasing admission standards will simply select students who have learned to conform well to the outdated educational system and will not help, but in fact, might even inhibit the ability of colleges and universities to respond to societal needs. This is the route taken by most "prestigious" institutions. Their graduate students perform well in the "system" but aren't educated to significantly help the nation respond to the foreign challenge on our industries.

Sponsoring remedial work for under-prepared students will probably be useful in the long run if institutions don't get hung-up on requiring all students to be competent in subjects for which they have little use in their disciplines. There are a number of ways that this can be handled.

According to a March 1989 ABC News report by Bill Blakemore, there is a public elementary school in Indianapolis that allows students to be smart in their own ways. That is, it permits them to choose and play with whatever they are drawn toward, such as art, music, word games, geometric structures, etc. As a result, they develop confidence, which they take into other classes — the "spillover" effect.

At this school, all skills are given equal time and importance for every student, and the children are given the opportunity to develop their own unique skills and to be "smart" in some areas while learning that others are "smart" in other areas.

One technique used at the school is group learning: students are asked to cooperate in figuring out a problem rather than compete for a grade in isolation. Not only is it more fun, according to the principal, but it is the natural way to learn to take advantage of each other's different abilities.

If universities would capitalize on the areas in which these students excelled in grades K-12 and attempt to improve these skills while, at the same time, expose students to other aspects of the curriculum, the entire selection and teaching process would have to be revised. We can see no disadvantage in a greater use of non-graded, interdisciplinary courses for much of what colleges and universities expect students to take for their general education. For example, by understanding the basic principles of music, one can understand and appreciate a symphony. By understanding a few basic principles of physics, one can understand many of the laws of the universe. Is it necessary to complete an entire music appreciation course to be a well-educated individual? Or is it more important that students develop skills in reading, writing, cooperating, listening and developing morals and ethics while increasing their abilities in genetically endowed "smart" areas?

Universities may wish to experiment with such a design. Maybe students should be graded only in their major, while having to show only an appreciation and understanding in related areas.

As we mentioned under Deming's second point, we believe each student should be required either to take a comprehensive course or to have a comprehensive orientation to the "society" of campus life. Freshman orientation courses appear to increase student retention, since students develop better study habits, learn the value of a liberal education and become aware of campus rules.

The development of measurement techniques for testing student knowledge and institutional performance is a good idea if the techniques are used to measure how well the systems and teaching strategies are working. Testing can be dangerous if its purpose is to measure content and reward institutions that use only traditional teaching and assessment methods. It should be noted, however, that *states are pressing campuses to live up to minimum expectations. It's like what happened when the American public got fed up with the automobile industry for turning out cars with defective brakes and rattling doors. Our equivalent for products this shoddy is students who take out guaranteed student loans and don't show up for class, athletes who don't pass their courses, and graduates who can't write clear sentences* (Edgerton 1986, p. 5). Higher education must convince the public that a quick cure is not possible, and that a long-term solution is needed with the vaccine being methodically designed innovative systems.

Routine testing doesn't indicate quality

Routine testing within courses doesn't reliably indicate quality. Testing may cause boredom and fatigue among the faculty. We recommend, therefore, that the administration and faculty work to establish a system for random testing in every course by outside evaluators. Such a mechanism would evaluate faculty members and students as they relate to the system they're using, and the long-range plan and mission of the institution. Furthermore, students should be tested according to their learning styles (Schmeck 1983, p. 385). The administration should seek the necessary funding for such a testing program, which should be linked directly to the faculty professional development program and student assessment program.

Ideally, a university should match the teaching styles of professors with the learning styles of students, since this matching is as important as testing to ensure quality graduates. Teaching and learning styles and their implications for improving educational practices have been addressed by Claxton and Murrell (1987). Every university faculty member should attend a workshop on teaching and learning styles to make them more sensitive to individual differences in students. To the extent possible, each university should test and evaluate each faculty member's teaching style and each student's learning style. When teaching and learning styles are properly matched, effective education is more likely.

Evidence suggests that success and retention are linked to good advising, counseling and assessing (Claxton and Murrell 1987). Further evidence suggests that mentoring is also very important. New students should be completely assessed before being advised into courses and curriculums. Since advising, counseling and assessing are so important, we recommend that every university consider the most efficient and effective way to implement these services.

By complete assessment, we also mean working with students individually to determine their financial needs and maturity levels. A cooperative education encounter might be prescribed to permit students to work part-time to pay for their education while they mature. We rigorously support a dynamic cooperative education program and active internship components for universities.

To ensure high-quality graduates, the administration and faculty should constantly ask (1) Who is responsible for the quality, assessment, advising and counseling of incoming students, and who will ensure their placement into the proper courses and curriculum? (2) Who is responsible to ensure graduates are competent and faculty members are current?

In the previous chapter we gave an example where an accurate class schedules could not be produced even after repeated inspections to achieve quality. Quality cannot be inspected into the product. The system for producing the class schedule was so cumbersome and out of control that despite people trying their best to produce a good product the end result was "junk." When the "system" was improved, the same good people produced an excellent product without the frustration and need for inspection.

Another example of not being able to build in quality with inspection: A university president approved hiring an individual as a distinguished professor, whose qualifications were among the finest in the discipline. The professor was to teach during a summer session but the president forgot he had approved the hiring and gave the vice president for academic affairs a directive to do another search for the position. The vice president told the dean; the dean told the chairperson; the chairperson told the vice president of human resources; the vice president of human resources told his administrative assistant to submit an advertisement. The administrative assistant, upon examining the file, wrote the following memo to the vice president of human resources:

"I have several communiques regarding this subject which have left me confused. I have the president's approval of (date) approving the hiring of Dr. X as long as it is in accordance with the appropriate contractual requirements. I have a memo from the dean asking that I advertise the position. I have the department's recommendation to hire Dr. X for the vacancy which includes a statement that Dr. X has already approved the dates and times for the classes. And, finally I have a memorandum from the vice president for academic affairs to the president stating that he has been in contact with you regarding this activity.

"Please advise if:

A. I should advertise this position again;

B. I should advertise this position in our service area; or,

C. I should prepare the employment package to appoint Dr. X to this vacancy?"

This needless repetition and confusion could have been avoided if someone had gathered the intestinal fortitude to inform the president he had already approved the position. Better still, the president should have had an information system that indicated such an approval had been granted. How many tax dollars were wasted when everyone went scurrying about trying to reinspect their work?

The following policy statement, an excellent example of how a faculty curriculum committee violates Deming's third point, was forwarded to the academic departments regarding the routing of new or revised courses through the curriculum committee. It should be noted that the curriculum committee had been accused of delaying the progress of new and/or revised courses.

1. Department chairperson sends course to Curriculum Committee chairperson, with a cover sheet signed by the dean.

2. The chairperson sends course outline to editing and library committee.

3. Editing and library committee interact with department chair or contact person.

4. Department returns course to editing with necessary changes.

5. Editing committee gives corrected copy to the subcommittee chair.

6. The subcommittee chair gives course to the Curriculum Committee chair to prepare copies for subcommittee.

7. The subcommittee chair calls department chair and puts course on the subcommittee agenda.

8. Upon action by the subcommittee, the item is forwarded to the Curriculum Committee chair who duplicates and distributes copies and places the item on the agenda for the Curriculum Committee.

9. Upon Curriculum Committee approval, the item is forwarded by the chair to the vice president for academic affairs.

The routing should have read:

1. The department chairperson sends course to the Curriculum Committee chairperson, with a cover sheet signed by the dean (if the format is not appropriate, the dean should not approve the course).

2. The chair distributes the course to the appropriate subcommittee.

3. Upon action by the subcommittee, the item is forwarded to the Curriculum Committee chair who duplicates and distributes copies and places the item on the agenda for the Curriculum Committee.

4. Upon Curriculum Committee approval, the chair forwards the item to the vice president for academic affairs.

Chapter 4:
Long-term relationships

Most purchasing decisions made in higher education are similar to those of other industries. Even the acquisition of staff is not significantly different. The one "purchase" that's unique to education is the student.

Students select institutions for many reasons, such as the tuition, reputation, location, etc. Ideally, all students should have the necessary skills to begin college level courses, but in reality, many fall short. Therefore, every institution should assess all incoming students for proper placement. The faculty should know the quality of their incoming students. Upon request this information should be provided.

The faculty and administration should work closely with the school districts and community colleges in areas from which they attract most of their students. Each institution should work with its "suppliers" (K-12), so they will better provide materials (students) suitable for a desirable product (graduate). This approach provides the institution with students with known educational backgrounds, including teaching and learning styles, who will more likely be able to complete their studies successfully. (Since most experiences in the educational system consist of traditional lecture and assessment techniques, we will refer to those students who respond well to this style of teaching and testing as having a high conformity index. Those who don't learn or test well by such techniques will be denoted as having a low conformity index.)

If the same philosophy were applied to branch campuses that are separated geographically and serve different student populations, then the "suppliers" (high schools and community colleges) might differ substantially. As a result, the chance of receiving students with inappropriate qualifications would increase. Branch campuses serving different student populations should be treated as separate functional entities that must establish their own systems.

Many aspects of continuing education are considered separately from other academic units. Continuing education departments usually have to be financially independent. As a result, most units of continuing education don't have the same strict standards in student selection as the typical academic department. By the same token, certain continuing education units cater to students who have graduated from universities and represent more highly desirable "products," and probably represent a high conformity index.

By providing continuing education to teachers at school districts supplying the most students, institutions should find higher quality students entering the system. This continuing education should also encourage long-term relationships based on loyalty, trust and understanding. With better teaching faculty, local grade schools and high schools should improve the quality of their graduates. Parents, taxpayers and industries should see the benefits, which will result in greater support for education and participating institutions.

In matters other than students, each institution should move toward a single supplier in such areas as equipment repair, institutional janitorial services, book store inventory and so on. This would help guarantee that the institutional facilities will be clean, the equipment in good working order, and that the book store and central stores do not have a large inventory. Working with single suppliers requires the administration to have the authority to order items and services quickly without the necessity of bidding. Funds used to maintain a large inventory of books and materials that might become outdated are lost money.

Most public institutions require that certain equipment be placed on bid to ensure that the "best" price is obtained. In theory this is admirable, but in practice it can become a nightmare for colleges and universities trying to establish a quality teaching environment (see below for examples). By placing items on bid, the chance for institutions to develop close working relationships with suppliers is diminished. A long-term relationship based on loyalty and trust is not possible through such a process. Furthermore, the bureaucracy necessary to oversee and control the bidding system on a state-wide basis probably doesn't save taxpayers much money, if any, especially when quality is considered.

When supplies and equipment are required, the university should write locked-in specifications. The following case studies show what happens when business is awarded solely on the basis of price.

Case Study: Management without leadership

The Computer Services Center director had all of her systems finely tuned. However, when asked by a dean to request a minor piece of equipment so a seminar could take place within two weeks, the director gave all the reasons why such a request could not be honored: it did not meet with her requirements! The equipment could have been purchased at a local store, possibly for $100 over a bid, but the benefit derived from the seminar could have saved the university at least $500,000 to $1 million a year over the next five years. The director managed the "system" well but had no leadership ability. How much would the lack of leadership cost taxpayers?

Case Study: Send in the clones

The business school dean and chairpersons submitted a large order for IBM personal computers that were to be installed in a new laboratory and used extensively by business administration majors. The order was submitted to the vice president for finance, who followed state guidelines and submitted the specifications for bid. The lowest bidder was for a clone that was completely "compatible" with the more expensive IBM.

Two years later the PC's are still not functioning properly and students and faculty are irate. In addition, the laboratory is being used for continuing education activities for the public, and on virtually every occasion the computers don't function properly. How much does the institution's reputation suffer when this occurs?

This waste could have been avoided if either the dean or the vice president for finance had written restrictive specifications so the proper equipment could have been obtained.

Case Study: Real deal on chalk and grade books

At one state university the purchasing agent obtained a "real deal" on one of the simplest, most basic items — chalk. He bought plenty. When the chalk reached the professors, there was a level of general unhappiness usually reserved for the assignment of offices and parking spaces. The chalk was too soft, did not erase well, and lasted only about one-third as long as the "more expensive" chalk.

The same institution permitted the purchasing agent to secure a large quantity of grade books. These were nicely designed for elementary school use with five-day week attendance records, small class seating charts and summaries for nine-week grading periods. The university had, however, large classes, evening sessions and 15-week semesters!

In both examples, the distance between the purchaser and user of the items placed the purchasing decision in the lap of an individual who could not differentiate between suitable and unsuitable goods. With quality not considered, the decisions were logically made on purchase price alone.

The problems could have been avoided if there had been a close working relationship between the purchasing agent and a quality-driven single source supplier.

In the School of Science, Management & Technologies (SM&T) at Edinboro University of Pennsylvania we are beginning to address Deming's fourth point in a variety of ways. We are writing tight specifications for equipment that would otherwise have to be bid to less desirable vendors. We are instituting a "science" newsletter to the local high schools to increase our image, to provide the science teachers with experiments for their classrooms, and to advise students who show interest in a college education. We also instituted an SM&T informational day for the high schools that act as our "suppliers." We're working closer with our school of education, and several professors in SM&T are conducting workshops for high school science teachers. We are also involved with a major foundation in recruiting and maintaining minority students who seek to major in one of the programs in SM&T. In addition, we are beginning to establish mentoring programs for school districts, community colleges and within our university. We also are producing "2+2" articulation agreements on the program level with the community colleges that act as major suppliers (see below for an example).

As a result of our science newsletter, a local high school requested that one of our physics faculty teach an honors section of our beginning physics course at their facility. They were not only willing to pay for the service, but they also requested that we grant university credit for the course — what an incentive for these high school students to enter Edinboro University!

The first SM&T high school informational day resulted in 500 students, teachers and counselors visiting our campus. The students participated in "games" (statistical, computer, geography, robotics, etc.), lectures, laboratory experiments and other university functions. Some departments had the students compete for prizes. We collected their names, addresses and telephone numbers, as well as their areas of interest, and will do follow up studies through our office of institutional research.

Many quality processes and systems are either free or inexpensive to establish. For example, establishing mentoring programs for local high schools and community colleges involves a community service function on part of the faculty and better students, and reimbursement for local travel and usually a meal. Establishing a mentoring program for students who have a tendency to miss SM&T classes involves collecting the class attendance records daily and having work-study students in the dean's office call these students and have them report to the dean. The dean, after instilling the "fear of God" in them, assigns a mentor. We are just beginning the mentoring process in SM&T and within a few years we will do follow up studies through our office of institutional research.

An example of a "2+2" program articulation agreement with a community college that acts as a major supplier to EUP follows.

A " 2+2 " Program Articulation Agreement.

AS in CHEMISTRY

By successfully completing the courses in Freshman and Sophomore Years (Column 1) at the Community College of Allegheny County (CCAC), the student will receive an Associate of Science Degree in General Studies (Chemistry).

COLUMN 1

First Semester

Course #	Title	Credits
ENG 101	English Composition 1	3
MAT 201	Calculus 1	4
	Social Science Elective	3
CHM 151	General Chemistry 1	4
	Humanities Elective (Speech)	3
		17

Second Semester

ENG 102	English Composition 2	3
MAT 202	Calculus 2	4
PHY 221	Physics for Engineering & Science 1	4
CHM 152	General Chemistry 2	4
	Elective	3
		18

Third Semester

MAT 250	Calculus 3	4
CHM 201	Organic Chemistry 1	4
PHY 222	Physics for Engineering & Science 2	4
	Humanities Elective (Philosophy)	3
	Elective	3
		18

Fourth Semester

CIS 124	FOTRAN Programming	3-4
CHM 202	Organic Chemistry 2	4
PHY 223	Physics for Engineering & Science 3	4
	Humanities Elective (Art or Music)	3
	Social Science Elective (Sociology)	3
		17-18

TO BS in CHEMISTRY

By completing the Junior and Senior Years (Column 2) at Edinboro University of Pennsylvania (EUP) the student with the Associate of Science Degree in General Studies will receive a Bachelor of Science Degree in Chemistry.

COLUMN 2

Fifth Semester

Course #	Title	Credits
SC 250	Quantitative Analysis	4
SC 530	Physical Chemistry I	4
SC 321	Inorganic Chemistry OR	
SC 421	Advanced Organic Chemistry	3
	Humanities Elective	3
HP	Health Elective	2
		16

Sixth Semester

SC 531	Physical Chemistry II	4
SC 533	Polymer Chemistry OR	
SC 450	Instrumental Analysis AND	
SC 534	Advanced Chemistry Lab	3 or 5
	Social & Behavioral Science Elective	3
HP	Activity Elective	1
GL 103	Reading German OR	
RL 103	Reading Russian	3
		14 or 16

Seventh Semester

SC 321	Inorganic Chemistry OR	
SC 421	Advanced Organic Chemistry	3
	Social & Behavioral Science Elective	3
	Electives	9
		15

Eighth Semester

SC 533	Polymer Chemistry OR	
SC 450	Instrumental Analysis AND	
SC 534	Advanced Chemistry Lab	3 or 5
	Electives	12
		15 or 17

Chapter 5:
Improve constantly

Deming (p. 49) believes quality must be built in at every step, especially the design step. This is true for every program, academic or non-academic.

To meet the changing needs of society, institutions must review and develop new programs, and improve existing programs and their delivery. Regular five-year program reviews and constant use of a departmental curriculum committee and an external advisory group will help such efforts. Such constant improvement efforts will require responsibility and commitment from a dedicated administration. Without an administrative commitment from the highest level, constant improvement will not occur. The top administration is in the position to define the improvement of quality, build a consensus around it, and allocate resources such that everyone in the institution can see that quality improvement does pay. The deeds from the top administrator must reflect an open and aggressive commitment to improve quality as an institutional necessity.

Administration and faculty should strive to adjust the times for classes so the room use rate is over 85 percent. Institutions should be able to offer classes from early morning until late at night, including weekends. Departments should be encouraged to provide self-instructional courses and telecourses. Such service should be available at any time during the year. Faculty, staff and administrators should, together, establish guidelines for quality in education.

Most universities offer classes in which students are tested, and use various mechanisms to evaluate faculty and managers. Unfortunately, in some cases, academic departments disagree as to what should be taught, in what manner and to which class. They also disagree about how students should be tested. Neither do faculty and management always cooperate in delivering educational services and evaluating faculty and administrators.

The entire environment must provide a means by which trust among different units in the institution can develop. Conversation among different disciplines and between faculty and administration, development of interdisciplinary courses, and a comprehensive general education program, can be achieved only in such an environment.

Mere allocation of money won't ensure quality, though mechanisms for providing incentives and proper rewards for quality improvement must exist. The improvement in quality is a cultural transformation based on vision and resources. But allocation of resources, monetary and non-monetary, requires careful and thorough planning and design, in which quality is built in.

Improving the process requires better allocation of human effort. Using human resources according to individual talent and without regard to hierarchical status develops the best product and makes the process more cost effective. But this requires situational leadership, which can be considered a threat by insecure managers because *"the assignment must be made without regard to hierarchical status, responsibility for the problem at hand, or seniority level within any particular agency or department. This approach has been shown to successfully break through such traditional organizational obstacles to innovation as 'group think' and 'analysis paralysis' in a wide variety of public sector organizations"* (Agor 1989).

Quality must improve constantly and become a way of life. "Putting out fires" does *not* improve the process, it only puts the process where it should have been in the first place. Improvement occurs little by little, step by step. It starts at the beginning of the design. The intent must be translated into all tests and evaluations and all of the institution's daily operations so each service is a little better than before and each graduate is better than those in the past.

We agree with Tom Peters (1988, p. 566) when he questions managers at the end of each working day: *"What exactly and precisely and explicitly is being done in my work area differently from the way it was done when I came to work in the morning?' The average manager starts each day as an expense item... not a revenue enhancer... What exactly, precisely, have you changed today? What precise bold goal is that change connected with? Ask yourself. Ask everyone, junior or senior, with whom you come in contact this very day. Repeat daily for the rest of your career!"* This same question should be asked of each faculty member and each administrator at the end of each working day.

To ensure constant improvement, academic departments should have ongoing blue ribbon committees on general education, professional development, mentoring, long-range planning & resource allocation.

Chapter 6:
Institute on-the-job training

Most university employees don't appreciate the wide variety of services that are essential to maintain a university. In many institutions the recruitment office often recruits without input from academic departments. Most institutions budget on a "blue sky" request basis, thus nullifying the input of those involved in the actual instruction. Most development offices raise money with little input from the academic departments and don't enlist the help of deans and department chairpersons in fund raising.

Although administrators of student services and academic affairs may work in the same office areas, they don't often coordinate "student services" and "academic services," an act that could help students attain their goals.

Deans understand the academic departments within their schools, and they might even understand how the schools fit into the mission of the university. But they usually don't understand the role of other university services, such as the security department, health services and janitorial services. Department chairpersons make a case for additional resources for their units without understanding the overall functions of the dean, the school and the many service departments. Faculty members concern themselves with teaching, and to much lesser degrees with student advising, research and community services. Any attempt to modify a curriculum to change the product is usually looked upon as a threat, rather than an improvement. The university setting is often, therefore, a Tower of Babel.

To change such isolationist attitudes, we encourage regular training for all university employees to inform faculty, staff and administrators of the functions of all offices. This should include everything from recruitment to the actual awarding of the degree; from housing to procurement and accounting; janitorial services to food services and financial aid; from the president's office to the registrar's office.

Many educational institutions tend to view "training" as something which we "do unto others" and think little about anyone "doing unto us." Our focus on educating students blinds us to the fact that we need also to educate, develop and train ourselves and our staff to continually improve. For example, the increasing computerization of universities often occurs with little training for those who will be operating the equipment, and so we permit individuals to sink or swim according to their own abilities. Often we find that this occurs with great waste of expensive equipment and valuable time and energy. With proper orientation and training, we might effectively combat techno-diseases such as "computeritis" and at the same time add enjoyable and challenging aspects to a person's job. Expenses, however, are associated with the training. Universities, as other organizations, must accept training costs as an investment that will pay off in the long run.

The development of university employee training programs brings other benefits. Training could be developed to allow all members of the university to understand better the relationships among different divisions and the roles offices play in the university's mission. This type of training would reduce the bureaucratic run-around given to students and others requesting information among different offices. Administrative offices in universities often challenge the skill of federal bureaucracies in "passing the buck." It is not atypical for students to be passed from office to office without receiving answers to routine questions.

It's easy to imagine the practical improvements to a system when employees are provided with training — training to learn particular jobs, orient employees to the university and learning new technologies — it simply make sense.

A university is a particularly sensitive setting in which to "train" members of an organization. Most individuals come to their positions with impressive credentials and years of education. The question of how one learns to teach has only recently been seriously addressed, because in the past we assumed credentials were the only prerequisites to teach. But the institution is more than teachers; more than teaching. And although the faculty may be partially served by vigorous orientation and development programs on the campus, the education and development must also be extended to those who support the faculty. We must train those in staff positions. It is especially with these positions that a comprehensive training program will benefit both the individual and the organization.

When personal and professional development programs are adopted for the staff, greater pride in performance will result. Ideally, the training will extend beyond the knowledge necessary to perform a particular job to include opportunities for all staff members to be challenged to grow and to reach their full potential. Job enlargement and job enrichment approaches are admittedly more difficult to institute in union environments, but these should be investigated nonetheless. Educational institutions are just beginning to feel the squeeze caused by shortages in the labor pool. Professional secretaries and technicians are being recruited at some prestigious institutions of higher education (Administrator, Vol. 7, No. 23, p. 2). As the labor pool shortage intensifies and the leverage of these groups increases, they will demand more professional treatment and concomitantly greater control over their functions. The training will, most importantly, allow them the opportunity for "mastery of task" (Hummel 1982, p. 108).

If the educational institution is comprehensive in implementing training programs, it will provide training for administrators that will help them recognize the importance of individuals having some control over the tasks with which they are charged. Training will teach administrators not to over manage or to over control the functions that are being performed. Administrators must learn to respect the individual's need to be the "master of his fate." Because of the complexity of the organization and the interdependence of all its members, it may be neither possible nor desirable for everyone to become totally independent; however, people must be as independent as possible.

If educational institutions use Deming's points to enhance jobs and positions, they may successfully increase employee job satisfaction while avoiding some of the pitfalls connected with breaching the other 13 points.

Case Study: I'm supposed to be where?

A dean receives a telephone call from a vice president who asks if he's coming to the meeting. The dean asks, "What meeting and where is it?" The dean is informed. He dashes off. He is 20 minutes late.

The dean had a "system" that permitted the secretary to do his scheduling. At the end of each working day the secretary transferred the schedule to the master calendar in the dean's office. At the end of the day, the dean checked his master calendar. But when the secretary went on vacation, she didn't teach the temporary helper to transfer the appointment schedule to the dean's master calendar because the temporary helper arrived only hours before the secretary left. The temporary helper couldn't be expected to perform a function she wasn't properly trained to do. (Neither can anyone be expected to perform a function for which he or she hasn't been educated.)

As a result, the dean was 20 minutes late to a meeting for which he was unable to contribute to. Likewise, four other university administrators wasted time waiting for the dean. Bringing the temporary worker on board a day or two before the secretary went on vacation, rather than a few hours before, might have prevented this problem. The total cost to the university for not educating the temporary secretary in a timely fashion greatly exceeded the cost of bringing the person on for a training session.

In the School of Science, Management & Technologies at Edinboro University of Pennsylvania we have instituted a series of training seminars to increase secretarial skills. In addition, we have instituted a series of seminars for the chairpersons and secretaries with other service units for a more complete understanding of each other's units. For example, chairs, administrators, faculty and staff are trained regularly in using the automated Financial Reporting System (FRS) on the VAX Office Information Service. Finance office staffers explain the data entries and reports (available to users on hard copy and campus-wide electronic databases).

When a faculty or a staff member attends a seminar/workshop and/or has developed particular skills that may be useful to others at the university, he or she is encouraged to conduct training sessions.

Chapter 7:
Adopt and institute leadership

"American institutions in general and those for higher education in particular have been coping, but they have not adapted to changing times, and are no longer perceived as leading. They are not perceived as leading, because, in fact, the institutions themselves, while being competently managed in most cases, are not necessarily themselves being led" (Giamatti 1988, p. 36).

Many universities are over-administered and under-led. They must make a commitment for all administrators to become leaders. Each administrator must become involved in publishing, doing research, seeking grant proposals, performing community service and teaching. Administrators must make it possible for the faculty to have pride in their functions, and must try to provide clean offices and classrooms, sufficient budget to maintain equipment and supplies, and opportunity for professional and personal development.

Administrators play a critical role in determining the success or failure of academic institutions; yet when the traits, skills and mannerisms of successful administrators are examined, commonalities in their style may not become readily apparent. Alfred North Whitehead (1953, p. 24) once wrote *"style is the exclusive privilege of the expert, the specialist."* One definition of "style" is "a distinctive manner of doing something." According to Giamatti, (1988, p. 36) *"(Leadership) is the assertion of a vision, not simply the exercise of a style: the moral courage to assert a vision of the institution in the future and the intellectual energy to persuade the community or the culture of the wisdom and validity of the vision. It is to make the vision practicable and compelling."* We make no distinction among different levels of administration — their styles may differ but they all have leadership abilities.

By diagnostic testing it is possible to locate administrators who have innovative abilities and who can be organized to facilitate innovation within the university. For example, it is well known that executives with high intuition tend to be better at innovation (Agor 1984). One well-known test for measuring an individual's intuition is the Myers-Briggs Type Indicator Test. When an institution appears to be stagnant and/or the leadership appears to be conventional rather than exciting, give the Myers-Briggs Type Indicator Test to identify administrators that may have the ability to execute change. Consider establishing a pool of administrators within the university to be responsible for solving problems and suggesting new approaches. Of course, the more traditional managers and faculty will tend to criticize either the group or their ideas; however, as time passes more and more of their ideas will find favor.

Since every organization has talent throughout, we recommend that the group almost immediately be expanded to include intuitive faculty and staff in addition to administrators. Such a group will create an atmosphere where innovation and research are encouraged, and a climate in which management and faculty will place a premium on decision-making.

Management leadership literature for institutions of higher education is extensive, and sometimes confusing and contradictory. Like leadership success in small business firms (Schermerhorn et al. 1985, p. 585), three general approaches emerge to explain what makes an effective higher education administrator. The first approach focuses on personal traits that effective administrators have more than ineffective administrators. The second explains effective administrators in terms of their interpersonal behavior modes. The third approach deals with a situational or contingency perspective, and explains effectiveness in terms of the conditions in which administrators work.

Administrative effectiveness is far more complex than enumerating a few selected personality traits or preferable interpersonal behavior modes. Success measured only against particular traits or behaviors may lead to mistaken conclusions that, as administrative responsibilities are broadened, a manager is a failure. The failure to obtain consistent results in identifying success leads us to focus on situational influences (Dressler 1986, p. 350) and how they relate to Deming's philosophy.

Administrative behavior that has enhanced performance in universities over the past several decades has depended largely on the situation. Effective leadership in one situation may be ineffective in another. Situational orientation suggests that an effective administrator is flexible enough to adapt to various situations or conditions.

Effective administrative leadership

An analysis of models depicting situational influences on administrative effectiveness reveals there is no universally accepted style of administrative leadership. In practice, administrators are seldom completely participative, supportive or directive. Many situational, personal and organizational variables influence administrative style and effectiveness. More specifically, the important variables and considerations that influence administrative effectiveness are the administrator's awareness of self, environmental parameters, characteristics of the institution, characteristics of the individuals in the academy, and the primary inherent motivational factors that prevail (Gibson et al. 1985, p. 393).

Effective administrators represent a fusion of many "types" and are, primarily, individuals who make things happen for the institution, faculty and students they serve. Successful administrators influence faculty and staff behavior, which in turn influences administrators' behavior and thoughts (Burns 1978, p. 9). It's not the intelligence, education, lifestyles or backgrounds of either administrators or faculty that constitute successful universities; it is the ability of administrators and faculty to deal effectively with each other. Successful administrators, however, have a style that makes it easy for meaningful interaction to occur (Peters and Waterman 1982, p. 81).

Regardless of the type of university, successful administrators create and sustain superior performance in two primary ways: (1) They encourage the faculty to provide superior educational experiences and the staff to provide exceptional support services for students. (2) They encourage constant innovation with new teaching strategies and research projects. Successful administrators realize their institutions must do these things well to sustain superior performance and a competitive market advantage for students (Peters and Waterman 1982, p. 13; Peters and Austin 1985, p. 3). But in reality it turns out that neither superior care of students nor constant innovation/research is built upon administrative genius, unusual operational techniques or mystical strategic moves or countermoves in the marketplace. Instead they are built upon the presence of committed people, whose commitment has evolved from a solid foundation of listening, trust and respect for the dignity and the creative potential of each person in the institution (Ruch and Goodman 1983, p. 43). Without exception, successful administrators realize this foundation of committed people establishes the winning team necessary for achieving the institution's goals and objectives.

In summary, successful administrators realize that organizational excellence within institutions of higher education depends on three variables: care of students, constant innovation/research and committed people (see Figure 4). In this model of excellence, we believe the one element that connects all others is effective administrative leadership.

Figure 4

Model of Keys to Organizational Excellence

Care of Customers

Constant Motivation

Administrative Leadership

Committed People

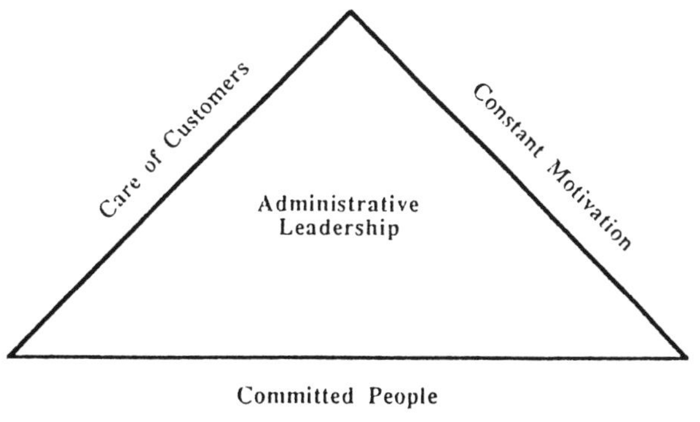

Adapted from Peters and Ausrin 1985, p. 5

Management versus leadership

In examining the leadership strategies of successful administrators, we find many academic institutions are over-managed and under-led. Managers may handle the daily routine efficiently, yet never question whether the routine should exist at all. In this regard, management and leadership differ profoundly, but we readily recognize that both are important. To manage means "to bring about, to accomplish, to have charge of or responsibility for, to conduct." Leading is "influencing, guiding in direction, course, action, opinion." The distinction is crucial. Managers are people who do things right and leaders are people who do the right things. Activities of vision and judgement enhance a leader's effectiveness; activities of mastering routines enhance a manager's efficiency (Hodgetts 1986, p. 515). Successful administrators may be good managers, but they must always be excellent leaders.

Leaders have a positive self-regard (Bennis and Nanus 1985, p. 65). They recognize their strengths and can compensate for their weaknesses, and tend to have the following five skills in common:

- They accept people as they are.
- They approach relationships and problems in terms of the present rather than the past.
- They treat those who are close to them with the same courteous attention they extend to strangers.
- They trust others, even if the risk is great.
- They do not need constant approval and recognition.

Successful administrators concern themselves with the institution's basic purpose and general direction, and are vision-oriented (Bennis and Nanus, 1985, p. 21). They do not limit their attention to the "how to's," but include the parameters of action, particularly caring for students, cultivating innovation, and nurturing and developing committed faculty and staff within the academy.

Successful administrators realize they don't have to be brilliant to be good leaders; but they know they must understand how people feel, and how to influence them effectively (Iacocca 1984, p. 53). For example, they're aware they will spend most of the working day dealing with people; the largest single cost in higher education is people; the most valuable asset of academic institutions is its people; and that all management plans are carried out, or fail to be carried out, by people. Therefore, they develop leadership strategies that deal with people.

One example of what may happen when a university lacks trust and leadership arose during a monthly meeting between representatives of the faculty union and management, when it took over 35 minutes to establish a meeting date. The scenario:

Union: Let's set a date and time for the next meeting.

Management: Good idea.

Union: By the way, at that meeting we would like to discuss why the previous meeting was cancelled by management without notifying us.

Management: Why? I thought you were submitting a grievance regarding that event?

Union: We are.

Management: But we are not permitted to discuss grievances at the local level, therefore, we cannot discuss this matter with you.

Union: Before this becomes a grievance, is it not advisable to discuss this issue?

Management: Yes. But we cannot negotiate.

Union: Are we not supposed to implement the contract at these meetings?

Management: Yes.

Union: But grievances are the direct result of the contracted not being implemented.

This posturing continued for 35 minutes, but eventually a meeting time and date were established. Needless to say, the rest of the meeting was just as productive. The cost to the taxpayers for these meetings is tremendous.

Such unproductive meetings could be avoided if leadership and trust existed rather than distrust. Many of Deming's points are violated in this case study, among which number seven's "Improve Leadership" is near the top.

Another pertinent example concerns faculty promotions. A contract with the union said the "... president could grant promotions to 5 percent of the faculty during any given year." Of the 400 faculty members, the president could have promoted 20 faculty members, but unlike the past, promoted only 15. At a meeting regarding this issue, union and management representatives spent nearly two hours discussing the contract language:

Union: The president only promoted 15 faculty this year. Is that true?

Management: I'm not sure.

Union: What do you mean you are not sure? I have the letters of promotion.

Management: Well, I guess that's right.

Union: Well, that's not 5 percent of the faculty.

Management: What's 5 percent of the faculty?

Union: Well, we have 400 faculty, and 5 percent is ...(pause as calculation is performed)... 22, or there about.

Management: But the contract states "... president could grant promotions to 5 percent of the faculty during any given year." It does not say that the president must grant promotions to 5 percent of the faculty.

Union: Yes, but he always gave 5 percent in the past, and we will grieve on precedence.

Management: If you must; however, the contract is clear.

Union: Does the president want to modify the guidelines?

Management: No, I don't think so.

After about two hours, both sides agreed that the union president and the provost would meet with the president to clarify the issue. How much does it cost the taxpayers of this midwestern university to permit such activities? Could not the money have been better spent on education? Open lines of communication and improved leadership could have prevented this problem.

Successful administrative leadership strategies

Leaders in institutions of higher education are people who inspire, by appropriate means, sufficient confidence to influence a group of individuals to become willing followers in the achievement of institutional goals (Bedeian and Gluek 1983, p. 494).

These leaders have the reputation for bringing change to the very foundations of the university and are viewed as creative change agents, not simply masters of basic routines. Successful leaders, in our opinion, share to a large degree four characteristic leadership strategies (Bennis and Nanus, 1985, p. 26):

- Attention through vision.
- Meaning through communication.
- Trust through positioning.
- Confidence through respect (see Figure 5).

Attention through vision

Attention through vision helps administrators create a focus for the institution. Successful leaders are acutely aware that virtually everything related to their responsibilities and the functions of their institution might be done faster, better, more reliably, with fewer errors and at a lower cost. They constantly look for and consider many possible answers. They are creative change agents because they want

Figure 5: Model of Keys to Organizational Excellence and Administrative Strategies

Care of Customers

Constant Motivation

Attention Through Vision

Meaning Through Communication

Leadership strategies

Confidence Through Respect

Trust Through Positioning

Commited People

to find a better way. But they seldom intervene to solve problems unless the problems can't be settled at a lower level in the organization. They believe in participatory management; in facilitating rather than in intervening.

These leaders always have an agenda, an unparalleled concern with outcomes. They are results-oriented individuals because results get attention (Dressel 1981, p. 83). Their visions or intentions are compelling and pull people toward them like a gigantic magnet. Their intensity, coupled with commitment, is exciting and contagious. Their vision grabs attention and encourages others to make a commitment to excellence for institutional achievement. They make all believe *"ideas beyond institutional means are not pipe dreams but the stuff of grant proposals"* (Brooks 1984). These leaders are, fundamentally, idealists who believe people can agree if they have broad goals and are future-oriented. These administrators are inner-directed and will not tolerate conditions that would prevent them from reaching their goals. If such conditions exist, they seek employment in another institution.

Successful administrators are known as movers. They have high goals and self-confidence, and they take risks and work hard in driving toward their goals. However, they always are aware of the political situation on their campuses, and in fact, encourage constructive political differences rather than a "sameness." At all times, they remain concerned about larger institutional issues.

Robert Kennedy made it popular, but George Bernard Shaw said it long ago: *"Some see things as they are and ask why? I prefer to see things as they might be and ask why not?"* Successful university leaders periodically consider their visions and the possibilities of what their institutions can become. Having done this, they commit themselves to the discipline necessary to make their visions a reality.

The following examples show vision and leadership in action:

- **It's not legal, but it's good:** A dean at an urban university discovered that the civil service personnel in his school had a high rate of sick day leaves. Upon investigating, he found this to be true in the entire state system. Upon further investigation he discovered that most employees took off to accommodate family schedules, such as taking children to school. Within his unit he established flex time. Within a year the absenteeism had dropped to near zero. Not only were employees happier, but so were faculty members since they received better service. The president asked how the school successfully reduced the absenteeism, and when told that flex time was introduced, he informed the deans that this was illegal in the state system (he also said he wouldn't report it if it was successfully implemented in other units as well).

- **Take a day off on me:** A dean of academic affairs at a large college informed the secretaries that if any of them found ways to improve the system, and if their suggestions were adopted by the college council, they would have an added vacation day. Within four months, five non-official vacation days had to be granted, but the improvement in the systems will result in tremendous savings.

- **Chairpersons can make a difference — a comparison:** During a meeting one chairperson complained he couldn't attract qualified faculty because the reputation of his department had deteriorated over the past decade due to inadequate funding for professional development.

Another chairperson (department of psychology) at the same institution had no trouble attracting qualified faculty: during difficult times he allocated travel funds only to faculty who presented papers. As a result, the reputation of his department remained high.

The first chairperson lacked leadership abilities and complained; the second chairperson was creative, and as a result, his department thrived. It should be noted that the chairperson of psychology offered training and social services to the United Way, an organization dear to the president's heart. Therefore, additional travel funds that became available at the end of the fiscal year were usually awarded to, among others, the department of psychology.

- **Chairpersons can make a difference in cost effectiveness:** After a period of declining enrollments at a northern university, all departments had few majors in their upper division courses except for one. The department chairperson had the foresight to assign most of his graduate assistants to the department's "killer" freshman and sophomore courses to tutor the students. As other academic departments lost the less-qualified students to attrition and became service departments, he enjoyed the prestige of having upper division majors during the good and bad times.

- **Just do it!** A director of student affairs was responsible for testing all incoming students and arranging interviews for all graduates seeking employment. He demanded fierce loyalty from his staff and encouraged them to generate programs that did not require approval from anyone, above the department chairperson. He refused to answer the memos of the vice president of academic affairs and the president — but they never threatened to fire him as his unit was highly successful in helping students to succeed. He did it; he did not ask permission.

At Edinboro University, the Myers-Briggs Type Indicator Test was taken by the dean, chairpersons and secretaries in the school of science, management & technologies (SM&T). The test results were shared and discussed so each was aware of his or her personality type and how that could affect working relationships.

Although the style of each administrator in the SM&T varies, each has made a commitment to determining the future of his or her respective unit, and has taken a leadership role in persuading other units within the university to do the same.

Each SM&T administrator has instituted leadership by involving his/her department in many of the prerequisite processes necessary for establishing quality: long-range planning, resource allocation, personal development, general education, facility remodeling, personnel evaluations, syllabus preparation, teaching/learning styles determination, new or improved program requests, course scheduling, etc. A winning team concept based on a systems approach to establishing quality was instituted, but the commitment was based on an all-personnel operation that included faculty and staff. Most of the decisions for running the academic departments were left to the department chairperson, including the internal reallocation of funds. Chairpersons were expected to perform, and their evaluations were based on how well they met the action objectives of the master plan they helped to prepare; i.e. management by policy deployment.

Each SM&T administrator approached problems in terms of the present and future, rather than the past. Within one year, each administrator has made a presentation and written a grant proposal, in addition to teaching and performing the aforementioned processes necessary to establish quality.

Chapter 8:
Drive out fear

"*The fear of failure has been internalized enough by most people; the organization need do nothing to reinforce fear as a motivational device. Threats and even consistent negative feedback increase caution and indirect strategies. There is already enough in work life to put us on shaky ground without management using fear as a tool. Most of us are already certain that our sins will be punished and our good deeds go unnoticed*" (Block, p. 129).

Deming (p. 28) stated, "*No one can put in his best performance unless he feels secure.*" Even the granting of tenure to a faculty member within an academic system does not remove the "fear" of administrative reprisal. Faculty and administrators may have a tendency to mistrust each other, and as a result, neither may be able to concentrate fully on the system that's needed to serve students and ensure quality.

Academic institutions must establish an open communication system to disseminate information to all faculty and staff as it becomes available to management. In addition, we recommend setting "fishbone" charts at various campus locations to elicit candid responses to problems. The results of the "fishbone" should be published in the institution's newsletter, and action should be taken to resolve issues/problems on either an institutional, school-wide, committee or administrative basis.

Not all conflicts can be resolved, but administrators should try to drive out fear by establishing trust through positioning, confidence through respect and meaning through communication.

Trust through positioning

Trust helps institutions function effectively, and although it may take years to establish, trust is necessary for effective management (Block 1987, p. 140). Like other administrative leaders, it's hard to imagine a successful institutional team without a reasonable degree of trust and credibility (Hayes 1983, p. 14). Faculty and staff will know trust is present, essential and predictable. Administrators should be predictable; their positions should be known.

People who don't trust administrators become their adversaries, and even serious negotiations won't turn the tide. According to Block, (p. 145) it becomes the ambition of those not trusted to destroy or convert his or her adversary. Sometimes, neither is possible and an understanding must be accepted by both parties.

Positioning encompasses a set of actions necessary to implement the vision of the administration. If vision is the idea then positioning will be the niche. For this niche to be achieved, administrators should reflect not only clarity, but constancy, persistence and reliability as well (Bennis and Nanus 1985, p. 46). By establishing position, and more importantly, maintaining continuity, administrators establish trust.

Successful administrators must maintain the ability to compromise. However strongly administrators feel about a goal, they should maintain the goal but yield on the methods and/or process. Administrators should avoid being locked into precedent or tradition.

One of the main keys to establishing trust through positioning is integrity, reflected in honesty and frankness, and properly clothed in tact (Dressel 1981, p. 104). Additional attributes help establish trust. Administrators should always attempt to accentuate the positive, maintain the desire to excel and be biased toward action.

Integrity must be established, and once compromised, can rarely be reestablished. Mark Twain suggested that once a cat sits on a hot stove, he will sit on neither a hot nor cold stove afterwards. Integrity in administrators leads to trust within the institution. As a result, administrators can facilitate the achievement of excellence.

Confidence through respect

Since successful administrators spend most of their time with others and are concerned with issues relating to people, a key factor in building confidence through respect is the creative deployment of self. Management should make administrative leadership a deeply personal activity because of the need for a positive self-regard.

Positive self-regard does not involve self-importance or self-centeredness. Leaders should trust themselves without letting their ego or image get in the way. Positive self-regard consists of three major components: knowledge of one's own strengths; the capacity to nurture and develop those strengths; and the ability to discern the fit between one's strengths and weaknesses and the needs of the institution (Bennis and Nanus 1985, p. 61).

Administrators should attempt to bring out the best in others by inducing a positive other-regard in the faculty and staff (Walker 1979, p. 3). Administrators should recognize and encourage latent talent, realizing that a person's inability to do one job doesn't mean the individual will be incompetent in all jobs. Confidence through respect would then become contagious within the institution, and fear could be eliminated.

David Whitten (1984), in an article "Effective Administrators: Good Management on the College Campus," described two types of leaders: charismatic and catalytic. Whereas the charismatic leader develops a loyal following, the catalytic leader fosters group solidarity and commitment. Administrators should attempt to nurture the better qualities of both.

Administrators should be change agents. They should effect change by working with groups, having empathy for fellow workers and open communication lines to reduce tension.

A vast array of conflict situations faces administrators in academic institutions. Frequently in the past these issues were approached with the basic assumption that conflict should be thoroughly analyzed, suppressed and eliminated. Conflict was viewed as being dysfunctional and time consuming. Society also generally reflected a fear of conflict, disagreement, hostility, antagonism and enmity (Maslow 1965, p. 185; Robbins 1974, p. 17).

Recently, however, successful administrators have recognized that in many instances conflict can be a sign of a very good organization. Successful administrators, therefore, are adept in conflict management, rather than "conflict resolution" (Thomas 1976, p. 889). These administrators realize conflict can have a number of benefits as well as costs.

Administrators must accept the notion that conditions other than peace and tranquillity can be positive for their institution — some conflict is therapeutic. They shouldn't fall into the trap of assuming their role is to eliminate tensions and promote harmony and cooperation.

The real challenge for top level administrators today is to learn how to respond positively and creatively to conflict at various levels and in the widely diverse arenas of a university. Universities are typically made up of individuals and operating units that compete for scarce resources. Administrators must recognize that every individual comes to an interactive situation with a different frame of reference, background, experiences and set of expectations (Darling and Cornesky 1987). With such differences, conflict of some magnitude will exist whenever interaction is necessary. In fact, it can be argued that the hallmark of a university as a complex organization is its high degree of differentiation (Lawrence and Lorsch 1969, p. 8).

Administrators should realize that eliminating conflict in an institution is as undesirable as it is unrealistic (Labovitz 1980). In short, managers must accept that some degree of conflict is an inevitable and important human process that can lead to creative results. Conflicts are likely to increase during times of change, and if those affected by conflict understand its processes and dynamics, they'll be better able to manage it. Administrators face conflict almost daily, and if managed creatively, these conflicts offer opportunities for institutional growth and broader understanding of organizational roles and responsibilities.

Academic departments themselves contribute to conflict in that they expect people who share different goals, time orientations, and administrative needs and philosophies to integrate their efforts into a cohesive whole, directed toward accomplishing the institution's overall goals. In the university's complexity and high degree of differentiation, communication among individuals, departments and support units can easily become distorted. Furthermore, people speak the language of their particular training and background, and often suspect the motives of those with different goals and objectives. In other words, the high degree of specialization within different departments creates isolation with no cross communication.

Differences between administrators and faculty in role expectations, goals and personality characteristics often contribute to interpersonal conflict. In universities, responsibilities are usually defined through traditional organizational charts and position descriptions. Unfortunately, such reflections of the organization often ignore the needs of individuals (Peters and Waterman 1982).

Conflict almost always exists when people or departments compete for scarce resources, particularly if one group gains at the expense of another. Conflict also arises when individuals or departments depend upon one another for fulfilling responsibilities, and when consensus is necessary for the organization to move toward its particular goals (Filley 1975, p. 9).

Effective conflict management then becomes essential, requiring a resolution of differences and a movement toward overall growth and development. To do this, administrators must deal with structural and interpersonal factors as well as the social conditions associated with conflict. In an academic unit, the process of managing conflict must, therefore, be considered as important as the end result.

To manage conflict successfully from the point of view that "together" we can solve "our" problem, managers must not assess blame; rather they should talk directly to those involved. An employee who displays anger toward another should be able to rely on the manager as a good listener. In other words, managers must make employees feel respected (Van Fleet 1984) and develop skills for managing conflict.

Skills of conflict management

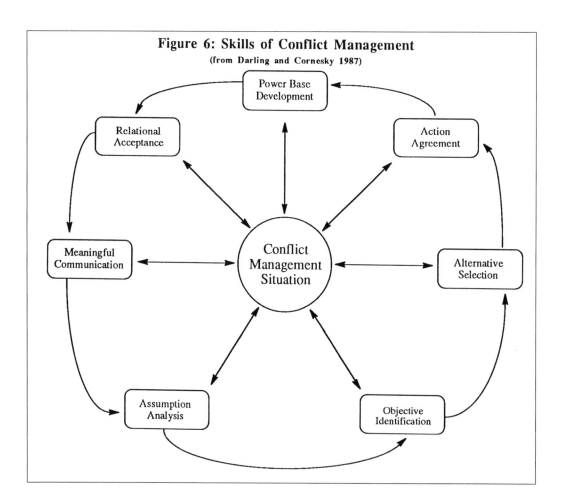

Figure 6: Skills of Conflict Management
(from Darling and Cornesky 1987)

Power Base Development

Relational Acceptance

Action Agreement

Meaningful Communication

Conflict Management Situation

Alternative Selection

Assumption Analysis

Objective Identification

There are seven steps in conflict management (Darling and Cornesky, 1987), but it may be more appropriate to consider the "steps" as "skills" in that administrators are seldom able to work with conflicts in a sequential step method. Usually what's required is a consistent, creative use of a situationally variable set of these basic skills. Both of these perspectives are reflected in Figure 6.

- **Power base development.** Before administrators invest time devising alternative solutions or insights into a given conflict, they should spend time helping each party ("side") to achieve a psychological power base on which to stand in relation to the conflict. Administrators must realize that individuals who feel threatened rarely think creatively about ways to resolve conflict.

If possible, the first step an administrator should follow is to hold one-on-one preliminary interviews with involved parties, giving each a chance to talk and the administrator an idea of the issues involved. This should let the administrator successfully interject him/herself into the process by structuring the context of the confrontation and facilitating the dialogue without provoking undue resentment.

Since administrators can influence the physical and social factors that provide the context for resolving the conflict, they should pay close attention to the neutrality of the meeting place, formality of the discussion and composition of the meeting.

Administrators are typically effective in resolving conflict between individuals when they serve as facilitators, rather than arbitrators or judges (Blake, Mouton, and Williams 1981, p. 238). As referees, administrators' responsibilities include establishing appropriate agendas and keeping the discussion on central issues. (Administrators should also restate briefly each participant's views periodically during the discussion, since redefinition will have the tendency to move the process from personalities to issues.)

During the "power base development" step it's important for administrators to establish and reaffirm the power base of both parties so neither feels so threatened that he or she overreacts.

- **Relational acceptance.** Conflict management requires a high level of trust for successful communication to occur. Conversely, when the level of acceptance and trust is low, communication typically is distorted and misunderstood, and responses are often emotional and irrational (Hall 1980, p. 80). Relationships aren't static, they're dynamic, and the level of acceptance and trust must be evaluated constantly (Morris 1981, p. 6). Since the foundation for successful conflict management is usually established in the development of the relational base, administrators must reflect honesty and sincerity in non-deceptive communications. Acceptance and trust are key concepts in developing a positive relational base.

Negative and judgmental feelings are often inevitable in conflict management situations, but administrators don't have to act on those feelings. Administrators must guard against emotional biases and prejudices, and maintain a mature, objective perspective (Fletcher 1966, p. 26). Administrators must realize that genuine acceptance begets acceptance, and estrangement begets estrangement. Trust and openness are also contagious. In creative conflict management this almost always involves giving another person the benefit of the doubt. When individuals are trusted, they usually do the right thing.

It's important for administrators to determine when conflicting parties are ready to communicate with each other. Premature confrontation often escalates conflict. Individuals must realize they are truly dependent on each other as they reach toward superordinate goals and seek common ground. This obviously assumes the issues to be resolved are objective and substantive, and do not merely reflect subjective and possibly irrational behavior. In this regard, administrators serve a vital role in helping to establish an objective and mutually agreeable definition of the problem.

- **Meaningful communication.** Administrative communication requires in-depth listening and the sending of positive and constructive messages (Tucker 1981, p. 184). Basic listening skills are both infinitely complex and profoundly simple. In conflict management these skills encompass sensitive perception and selective reflection.

Sensitive perception involves listening with intensity to what is and what isn't being said (Sanford 1973, p. 231). Administrators must be able to tell the difference between the medium and the message; between what's being said and the way it's said. Communication takes place in a variety of ways at these levels, and a successful communication process involves a total integrated circuit, encompassing feelings as well as ideas and facts. Sensitive listeners observe and listen at the same time for many different levels of communication, and determine the real message the person is communicating.

Sensitive reflection helps administrators decide the appropriate level of communication to which he or she can respond most constructively. People can control actions and words but not always feelings and emotions. It's not essential to respond to everything, but it's often important for administrators to repeat what they've heard because emotions and defense mechanisms frequently filter the hearing process (Ferguson 1980, p. 229). Another benefit may be a more finely focused message from the sender. Administrators cannot be passive participants in the conflict management communication process.

Administrators' perceptions should be subjective; thus, what's communicated should be stated as a subjective perception, not established fact. This gives the other person the room and right to have perceptions without requiring that someone be right and someone wrong. Adhering to such an approach helps administrators keep conflicting parties from becoming defensive and engaging in unnecessary arguments. Implicit in this approach is that administrators must have respect for the feelings, attitudes and thoughts of both sides.

Constructive communication makes it necessary to send "I" messages by which administrators describe how "I" feel rather than messages that blame, condemn, admonish or command. By using "I" messages, administrators give both sides the freedom to explain the situation without having to engage in an adversarial exchange.

- **Assumption Analysis.** Creative conflict management also includes the ability to identify and test for reality the assumptions of conflict participants. This is essential because it's at this point that reality focuses sharply on the inevitable assumptions people involved in the conflict bring to it (Hershey and Blanchard 1977, p. 176). The administration can analyze assumptions by asking what assumptions conflicting parties make. If the parties can't deduce which assumption is valid or invalid, the administrator should ask: Is it constructive or destructive for the participants in the management process to work with this assumption? If it's helpful to accept an uncertain assumption, then it is retained. If it gets in the way of creative conflict management the administrator should consider it invalid and take no action, at least initially.

- **Objective Identification.** In the conflict management skills noted above, administrators focus attention on the personal, relational, affective and cognitive dimensions of the conflict. They should also consider the more active dimensions of the conflict situation. Rather than asking in-depth analytical questions about what caused the conflict, we suggest that administrators must ask a more critical question: What should be accomplished in this situation?

Questions about the cause of the conflict often lead to more conflict, since it's usually difficult for conflict participants to agree on what caused it. It is typically more productive, therefore, to ask each participant in the conflict what his or her objectives are. In the final analysis, the goals must be identical. Administrators must arrive at a broad enough description of the total set of objectives so that an area of overlap can be established, i.e. points at which the objectives correspond. In addition, it should also provide another means of focusing on the superordinate goals of the university (Osborn, Hunt, and Jauch 1980, p. 380).

The concept of working together in the overlap areas is an important part of conflict management. It affirms that people have the right to their own goals and objectives, and that nobody has the right to manipulate someone else to work toward accomplishing his or her own goals (conflict with superordinate and organizational goals may be an exception). Nor is it necessary to convince a person to alter a set of goals to fit another person's.

When conflict participants work together in an overlapping area, trust, acceptance and understanding of each other's goals and objectives are broadened, and the area of overlap grows. Superior administrators are able to address specific, definable, measurable goals within the area of overlap. Once goals are established, administrators can find ways to reach them with individuals involved in the conflict.

- **Alternative Selection.** Alternative selection begins with brainstorming, where all ideas are identified without being evaluated. This process allows individuals involved in the conflict to respond with new ideas and evolve innovative possibilities. No negative factors should be introduced during brainstorming sessions (von Oech 1983).

Once participants have exhausted all possibilities, the criteria for selecting alternatives can be established, based upon the parameters of the situation and the priorities involved in decision making. The question can then be raised as to which alternative can best be achieved within the parameters according to a set of priorities.

In selecting alternatives, administrators should consider the risk versus payoff in each possible solution. Some individuals will choose low risk alternatives regardless of the payoff, while others tend to choose high payoff alternatives regardless of the risk. Truly creative conflict managers are able to evaluate the risk in comparison to the payoff and make a rational decision based on these two considerations. The risk and payoff can be identified by asking three questions: What is the best that can happen as a result of this alternative? What is the worst that can happen as a result of this alternative? What is most likely to happen?

- **Action Agreement.** After administrators have helped to identify objectives and select the best alternatives, they must establish an agreement among people involved in executing that decision. At the simplest level, that may mean rehearsing, orally or on paper, decisions that have been made, and identifying precisely what each person is going to do. At a more sophisticated and complex level, it may mean taking a systems approach to achieving the objective according to the method selected. This would include establishing specific times, events, accomplishments and goals according to the basic systems approach in administrative decision making. This approach should enable administrators and conflicting parties to know what's expected of them and when, and it gives administrators a mechanism for monitoring the development of the planned resolution.

Many academic institutions evaluate faculty annually until tenure is achieved, and every five years thereafter. Faculty evaluations usually include student, peer and administrative evaluation of performance. Most evaluations are done very subjectively or with instruments ill-suited for the task. Since faculty are usually evaluated with no reference to either professional or personal development programs, identified weaknesses aren't subjected to procedures for improvement. These evaluation procedures are usually based upon management by objectives, and they lead to the same evil as the evaluation of faculty, i.e. management by fear. As Deming says about such evaluation procedures (p. 102), *"The effect is devastating: It nourishes short-term performance, annihilates long-term planning, builds fear, demolishes teamwork, nourishes rivalry and politics.* He further states, *Merit rating rewards people that do well in the system. It does not reward attempts to improve the system."*

Money set aside for merit pay is usually an insignificant amount of the total budget. It's given to a few chosen individuals, and as a result, everyone else in the organization feels slighted. Merit pay is a very inexpensive way of getting most employees angry at each other and the administration. It should eliminated.

Eliminating "Management By Objective" (MBO) and substituting management by policy deployment is considered in greater detail in Point 11. Abolishing annual or merit evaluation systems is discussed further Point 12.

Meaning through communication

To be successful administrative leaders, managers must be able to relate a compelling image of a desired state of affairs, not only to faculty and staff, but to the entire university community (Peters and Waterman 1982, p. 67).

Most institutions are based on a set of shared meanings that define roles and authority, procedures and objectives. In the ever-changing environment of higher education, the "know why" is more important than the "know how."

In the School of Science, Management & Technologies (SM&T) at Edinboro University of Pennsylvania, we are developing a systems evaluation of faculty. Such a model could conceivably end up with a series of performance evaluations (students of faculty, students of courses, faculty of students, faculty of courses, peer evaluations, self evaluations, etc.) that would be associated directly with professional development and a concomitant evaluation of the working systems. Although in the conceptual phase, such a comprehensive, ongoing evaluation could reduce fear, since the perceived weaknesses of a faculty member would not subject him/her to dismissal, but only to professional development and a greater assurance of success. Furthermore, such an evaluation procedure would assist the administration in repairing the "systems."

Chapter 9:
Break down barriers between departments

All personnel must realize they are important to the success (or failure) of the institution regardless of their position. At the department level, this includes not only faculty, clerical and support personnel, but also employees who are within the physical confines of the department but whose administrative supervision is outside the department (e.g. custodial and maintenance workers). Further, students' contributions to the department should not be minimized, as they often provide insights that haven't occurred to the staff. Perhaps even more important, today's students are tomorrow's alumni and mentors.

A sense of "belonging" is critical. The department chairperson is usually the conduit through which information, decisions and recommendations move in and out of the department. Consequently, the chairperson is largely responsible for implementing strategies to develop a sense of belonging. These strategies should be applied to all constituencies whose activities impinge upon departmental operations.

Several strategies involve communications. For example, all personnel involved in the department's operation should believe their comments, suggestions and complaints will at least be listened to. This does much to foster the sense of belonging and can provide the chairperson with immediate, first-hand knowledge of problems or potential problems that could hamper successful department operation. It can also provide opportunities to strengthen and support activities that enhance department operations.

The department chairperson's authority or power varies considerably from one institution to another. In virtually every instance, however, one of the "powers" common to every department chairperson is the power to withhold information. Using this power is generally counterproductive. First, it may prevent people from efficiently carrying out their assignments, thereby detracting from successful department operations. And as faculty learn that information is being withheld (and they will), the critical sense of belonging will begin to erode. It is far better that access to all information affecting a department's operation be provided to everyone affected by that information.

In one instance, an academic dean requested that he be sent copies of the faculty union's newsletter so he could be kept informed of important issues. The following reply came to his office from a union representative:

"This office believes that this type of information should be shared in order to facilitate a better understanding of each other's position. You can recall the numerous times that we have requested that we receive copies of memos that vice presidents and deans send to the department chairpersons (members of the union). If we can agree that these memos above are copied to our office, *then* I will make the necessary arrangements to have the union's newsletter mailed to you."

In another example a dean sent out an agenda regarding the school's first meeting for the academic year. Among the items mentioned were "Retention, Promotion, and Tenure Criteria." Immediately, without checking on the content of the agenda item, a single member of the faculty, the long-established chairperson of the "Promotions Committee," responded with a memo stating, "the policies and procedures have established the criteria and instrument to be used in the evaluation of promotion... at this institution."

Furthermore, this individual, who obviously felt threatened, stated: "Individuals cannot incorporate other criteria or alter the weights assigned to the criteria without having the changes mutually agreed to..." In addition, the union president gave a warning to the dean on the subject of "Potential for Grievances and Unfair Labor Practice," which stated "... many faculty of the school ... have voiced similar concern to this office."

The dean's speech encouraged the faculty to observe the guidelines and to have union representatives conduct a workshop/seminar on the preparation of a portfolio that would facilitate the retention, promotion and tenure of the faculty in his school. (The speech, written several months before the union's apprehensive remarks, also encouraged the faculty to come together as a unit to discuss matters of concern to the school.)

Fund raising strategies

One good way to help break down barriers among academic departments is to get chairpersons and faculty involved in fund raising. Of course, faculty frequently ask, "Whose responsibility is it to raise money for my department?" Some presidents and vice presidents for development believe it's their function to raise money, not faculty and chairpersons. Many faculty and chairpersons might agree with this. Although there is no single answer to this question, one sure way to drive information between departments is to involve the faculty and chairpersons actively in fund raising and have them work closely with the office of development (Cornesky and Anderson 1987, p. 156).

Most colleges and universities have policies and procedures that coordinate private sector fund-raising. This is good because it can become embarrassing for individual departments, the office of development and the president if a funding source is approached by several departments from their institution. Development efforts, therefore, should be coordinated through the office of development, as officers are trained to prepare proposals and identify and secure private sector support by establishing a people network.

According to Thomas Broce (from "Fund Raising: The Guide to Raising Money from Private Sources," by Thomas E. Broce. Copyright 1979 by the University of Oklahoma Press), nine principles form the skeleton of a development program:
  • Institutional or organizational objectives must be established.

In Deming's first point we stressed the importance of long-range planning for the institution and the academic departments. In establishing a long-range plan (LRP), the faculty and administration establish and support a constancy of purpose; i.e.

mission. During the planning process many, if not all, departments receive the advice of a development committee, consisting of alumni, employers of graduates and individuals from corporations and industries that routinely support the institution.

- Development objectives must be established to meet institutional goals.

Since donors give to meet objectives, the department chairperson and faculty must demonstrate how resources will be allocated to meet institutional and departmental objectives. This in itself requires a consensus, which is good.

- The type of support determines the type of fund raising program.

The vice president of development should meet with the department faculty to explain the different sources of funding and help identify which are most appropriate for their objectives. Such meetings not only inform the development office what faculty members are doing and what they need, they also educate faculty to the complexities of fund-raising, especially in the highly competitive arena of higher education.

- The institution must start with natural prospects.

Well-established academic departments with many graduates have the advantage in that they may approach individuals and organizations that have given routinely in the past. When faculty and chairpersons contact corporations, foundations and potential individual donors, they will learn what the "world" thinks about the institution, its program and its graduates. Faculty may find the public's opinion to be frightening, and the result may be the crumbling of the ivory tower and a much-needed change in the curriculum.

- The case for the program must reflect the importance of the institution.

The university and departments must prepare case statements if they are to solicit funds. Case statements require a long-range plan and clearly defined objectives, especially at the departmental level.

- Involvement is the key to leadership and support.

The best fund raising efforts involve everyone; faculty, chairpersons, deans, advisory committees, the staff and the office of development. Participating in such efforts will also increase morale, as those involved will look upon the institution as "theirs" rather than just a place to work.

- Prospect research must be thorough and realistic.

The office of development must do the prospect research; however, if selected faculty and chairpersons are involved in the necessary disciplined procedures and processes, they will better appreciate the administration's efforts.

- Cultivation is the key to successful solicitation.

The office of development may assign this responsibility to the faculty, president, vice president, deans or advisory committee members. No matter who is responsible, faculty members may have useful information or contacts that would help the office of development identify prospects, therefore they should be included into the cultivation process.

- Solicitation is likely to be successful only if principles one through eight have been followed.

Fund raising model

Chairpersons should be actively involved in fund raising (see Figure 7), though close interaction between academic departments and the office of development is vital. What follows describes the role and function of the academic department in fund raising. The role of upper administration (president and deans) is well known.

Fund raising can be initiated in academic departments since most people who give to universities earmark their donations for a specific objective or goal. These are most clearly defined at the department level.

To best define the objectives and goals of a department, a long-range plan is necessary, since it will cause the department to identify its action activities as they relate to the mission of the school.

During the long-range planning process, departments should consider the findings of a community advisory committee and include the vice president of development and the vice president of research in its deliberations. Such protocol will give the vice president of development and vice president of research a chance to comprehend the needs and future directions of the department.

Academic departments must select their advisory committees carefully, choosing members from the community who are knowledgeable about fund raising. These people should be recruited and informed of their purpose. Members of the advisory committee should meet certain criteria:

- They should either know about the mission of the university and the department or be willing to learn.
- Their backgrounds should be diverse.
- They should represent a wide geographical area.
- They should be willing to give financial advice.
- They should either be proven donors to the department or be willing to give and allow their gifts to the department to be publicized.
- They should be willing to use peer pressure to influence others to give to the department.

The cultivation and selection of the departmental advisory committee may require solicitation from the dean, vice president(s), and/or president rather than the department chairperson, but the president's support of these individuals is very important. Additionally, it's helpful if a member of the department's advisory committee is also a member of either the dean's advisory committee or the president's governing board.

A department, working with the office of development and its advisory committee, should consider its mission statement, needs and objectives, and should prepare a case statement.

Guardo (1982) states, "*A university mission statement sums up the academic identity of the institution. It covers the type of educational institution the university is, the kind of educational philosophy it espouses, and the specific educational aims and purposes it seeks to fill.*" The department's mission statement must support the mission statement of the school and university.

The needs and objectives will result from the long-range planning process. The department should express each objective clearly and concisely in no more than two or three sentences. Each objective should have a price tag, priority and strategy for implementation.

The department's case statement should be prepared carefully and be approved by the dean, vice president for development and president before being published and distributed. The department's case statement should support the university's case

Figure 7: Fund raising model, including the active involvement of academic departments.

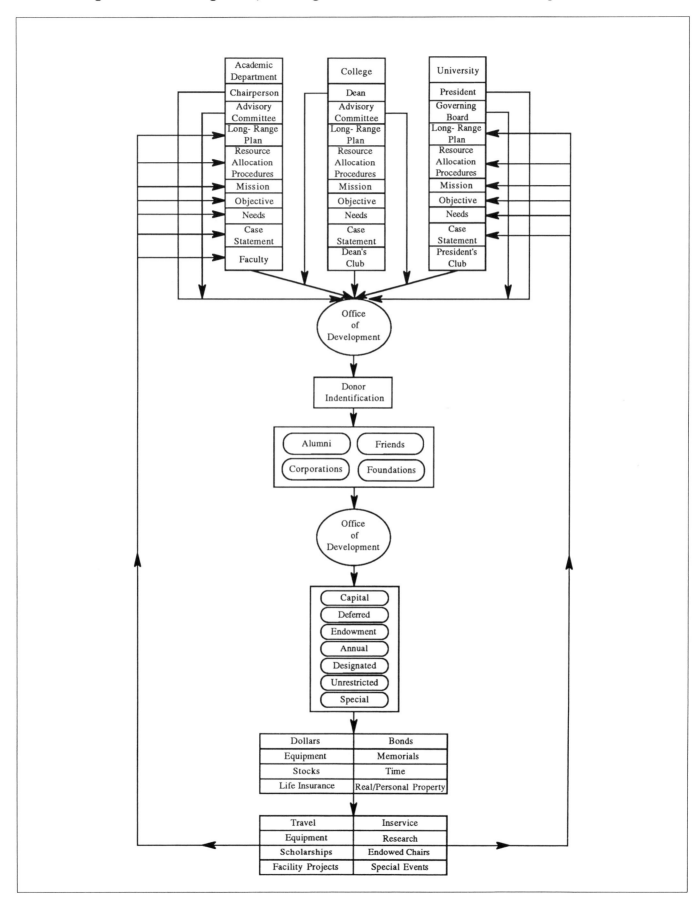

statement and goals. In this regard, each case statement should involve active input from the office of development, even in the initial phase.

Kunec (1982) notes, *"The case statement is a document that states the well-researched arguments that express an internal consensus on your organization's rationale for existence."* He suggests the case statement should contain six elements:

- A section on history and tradition that defines why the organization was founded and its philosophy and heritage. This section should include information on the department's mission.
- A description of the program and the services it offers to the community.
- A description of how the department intends to improve its current capabilities and how this will affect the community.
- A description of the faculty and the advisory committee.
- An invitation to others to participate in determining the future of the department.
- An outline of opportunities for giving, including time, resources and money.

As shown in Figure 7, the office of development will receive suggestions from the president, governing board and the Dean's advisory committee, as well as the department and members of its advisory committee. The office of development must coordinate this information and set priorities before the donor identification process is started.

Eventually, the chairperson and the faculty should assist in identifying and cultivating donors. This may include contacting alumni, friends, corporations and foundations interested in helping the department meet its goals. In addition, the vice president should work closely with the chairpersons to help them determine categories potential donors may be willing and able to contribute to.

In addition to involving the faculty and staff in fund raising, there are other ways to break down interdepartmental barriers. For example, we recommend that various academic and nonacademic departments offer seminars on the functions and successes of their units, and make these seminars available to the entire institution. People in accounting, purchasing, academic affairs, student affairs and the president's office should encourage regular seminars on the functions and successes of their departments as well.

People in recruiting, admissions, advising, counseling and teaching should work together to identify problems in students' academic preparation. They should be aware of problems with incoming students, their educational experience and the quality of high school graduates. If not, improperly prepared students will enter the system and will either require substantial remediation or drop out. In either case, there will be a substantial loss in human potential or revenue that could have been used to increase the quality within the existing system. Society pays for the loss one way or another. Teamwork among administration, faculty and supporting staff could eliminate these losses, or at least reduce them substantially.

Case Study: The great air conditioner fiasco

Two classrooms had to be converted into a robotics laboratory and an electronics laboratory, and new offices and storage areas were also needed. The classroom building where the conversion was to occur was notorious for very high levels of humidity and heat during the summer months, which would be detrimental to the new equipment. Therefore provisions for air conditioners were made for each laboratory.

Since the project was to be completed in late spring, the department ordered a number of air conditioners, which were delivered in May. Unknown to the academic department, however, the maintenance department was aware of the possibility that in two years the entire classroom building might be air conditioned. Maintenance, therefore, adopted a stalling tactic, feeling it might never need to install the individual air conditioning units. Maintenance proved correct in its guess that the classroom building would be air conditioned (although this has not actually happened yet). The net effect is that the laboratories have gone through two summers of adverse conditions, and the department spent $2,500 on air conditioners that have never been used. There is no way to assess how much the electronic equipment's lifetime has been reduced by exposure to the high levels of humidity and heat. The problems could have been avoided if all parties to the original plan had been clear about the timetable and individual responsibilities.

Although teamwork is desirable, it can be, according to Deming, a risky business. If a person helps another, he ... *may not have as much production to show for the annual rating as he would if he worked alone* (p. 64).

For example, a recruiting office may bring in an additional 1,000 students for a given academic year. However, if 750 of them aren't qualified to undertake the challenge of a university curriculum, they'll either require substantial remediation or drop out. By the same token, if an academic department raises its entrance requirements to ensure a better qualified major, the vice president/director of recruiting may object, since that might reflect on his/her ability to keep up with "production."

If an increase in student enrollment requires additional course sections, academic affairs may or may not have sufficient funds and/or time to locate instructors. If instructors are located, the facilities may not be suitable to house faculty or students. If faculty are required to teach overloads or exceedingly large classes, the production mentality will inhibit faculty morale, research and service; all of which will reflect poorly on the institution and the students. But the cycle can be avoided if meaning through communication (see Figure 4) eliminates barriers among staff areas.

Other ideas you can use

- **The flow of information:** A university president has monthly meetings at the chancellor's office with other CEO's in the state system. Upon returning, he calls a day-long meeting with his vice presidents and director of institutional planning to discuss with them in detail the results from the systemwide meeting.

That's a very good system. An excellent system would be to include the deans as observers of the discussion. A super system would include deans, chairpersons and the faculty senate executive committee as observers of the discussion.

- **Pooling resources:** The department of physics & technology needed a computer laboratory to support CAD instruction while the department of business & economics needed a similar laboratory for business and accounting courses. By pooling departmental budget resources the two departments were able to create a single laboratory that satisfied both their needs.

- **Service between units:** The speech department faced a critical deadline in producing a brochure for a summer workshop. They went to the public relations office and were told it would take two to three weeks to complete. Because the secretary of the speech department was aware of desk top publishing facilities in the physics & technology department, she contacted the chairman for assistance. He was able to help a graduate assistant from the speech department produce a camera ready copy of the brochure in one afternoon. The duplicating department then made the final copies the next day — total time required was less than 24 hours.

In the School of Science, Management & Technologies (SM&T) at Edinboro University of Pennsylvania (EUP) we've stressed the teaming aspect by instituting regular meetings between the dean and all chairpersons so information can be exchanged regularly. In addition, a process involving the faculty and chairpersons in long-range planning, resource allocation and professional development was instituted. Central to all this was the role of the department chairperson.

Once the long-range plan was approved, the chairpersons and faculty became involved in redesigning several facilities that were slated for remodeling. In addition, the chairpersons were involved in providing information necessary for the preparation of a case statement for presentation to private foundations. Several chairpersons, for the first time, became actively involved in soliciting funds for their department from the private sector and were successful! Other chairpersons are approaching their eventual fund-raising thrust by first establishing active community advisory committees.

To constantly improve the communication between and among the departments in SM&T, the office of the dean has instituted a newsletter, and a committee of SM&T faculty has instituted a bimonthly informal luncheon meeting.

Chapter 10:
Eliminate slogans

Management should, in a timely fashion, report to faculty, staff and students efforts to update equipment and facilities, improve the professional and staff development and the quality of education. This should boost morale.

The difficulty with slogans and exhortations is that they are directed at the wrong people (Deming 1986, p. 66). Management's supposition that faculty can improve their course grading without meaningful training, better prepared students or up-to-date equipment and facilities indicates a lack of leadership. They blame people rather than the system itself. For example, a management directive recommending that faculty improve grading techniques in courses showing "excessive" percentages of D's and F's is counterproductive. Such directives usually do not include systematic plans for improving grading but instead direct attention toward the names of staff members teaching the courses listed in the directive. The implication is that the quality of education improves by reducing the number of D and F grades.

Exhortations and slogans generate frustration and resentment (Deming 1986, p. 67). They indicate to the faculty that management is unaware of the barriers to faculty workmanship. Management needs to develop leadership qualities, learn that its main responsibility is to improve educational systems and remove defects within the system so the faculty can do a better job of teaching.

The immediate or short-term effect of slogans, exhortations or new goals may be improved quality and productivity, but without administrative leadership and the resulting interaction between faculty and administration, the improvement eventually ceases and regression ensues.

There has been great concern at Edinboro University of Pennsylvania (EUP) for the student advising system. The president assigned the problem to his faculty advisory group for study. The committee was charged with recommending improvements to the system. Under the advising system that was used, student dissatisfaction was blamed on poor faculty advising and a lack of meaningful faculty-student communication outside the classroom. "Faculty are not available for advising," said some of the students. Dissatisfied faculty advisors blamed the problem on many students who do not use the advising system until they are either near graduation or in danger of academic dismissal. In either event the assumptions — by faculty and students — were that the users were in control of the advisory process and were to blame for its inconsistencies.

In past years, administration responded to complaints about the advisory system by sending directives to faculty indicating they should make adequate time available at their offices so quality advising could take place. Students were directed to seek advisement well in advance of preregistration. In either case, the implication was that faculty and students were to blame for problems in the system, and therefore had to take new initiatives to improve it.

The advising system is the responsibility of management. If the system is stable (in control) and is not satisfactory to users, it's management's responsibility to improve it. If the system is not stable, there can be no reason to believe it will perform in any predictable manner. An unstable system must be changed, and only management has the resources available to change it.

The Faculty Advisory Group recommended that a noted consultant be secured to analyze the student advising process. The consultant's report indicated that a lack of communication at all levels was evident, and that the advising system was, at best, fragmented and inconsistently used by administration, faculty and students. Faculty expected another directive concerning faculty advising, but no directive was issued.

Based on the consultant's recommendations, the vice president for academic affairs selected a team of faculty to develop a prototype for an advising procedure and design a handbook to help students and faculty to better understand the advising process. Management exercised its responsibility opened a line of communication between administration and faculty. The prototype is still being designed and the team is now awaiting feedback from colleagues. The lines of communication are slowly being put into place. The fruits of administrative leadership may result in an advisory system that is stable and can be easily used by faculty, students and administration.

Additional feedback and evaluation will be important to determine the stability of the advisory system. If the system is stable, administration must take steps for continuous improvement. If the system is unstable, administration must effect change in the new system. The causes of low quality advising belong to the system and thus lie beyond the power of faculty and students.

Chapter 11:
Eliminate quotas, MBO

The administration should eliminate faculty quotas, even though public higher education is obliged to deliver a good education to a maximum number of students at a reasonable cost.

An institution's resource allocation procedure should not be based on the cost per student credit hour alone, although this is an important consideration. Each employee of the institution should remember the effect that productive, competent graduates have upon employers. Likewise, everyone should remember the effect that satisfied students and their parents will have in spreading the news about the programs. In other words, the cost per student hour may be important in setting up the initial resource allocation procedure, but the quality of the graduate is most important in maintaining the program.

If the vice presidents construct a resource allocation formula for each department without input from the dean of the school and the respective department chairpersons, they will most likely attempt to manage by figures alone. Vice presidents don't usually have the knowledge necessary to deal with the problems of delivering quality education in all departments. In most cases, the vice presidents' answer to increasing productivity is to enlarge class sizes.

If a resource allocation formula is used to drive the long-range plan and if it has the input of faculty, chairpersons and deans, the formula will help identify areas requiring resources. However, if the formula is used simply to increase productivity without placing quality and pride of workmanship first, the following chain reaction could occur:

- The institution's resource allocations are based solely on cost per student credit hour.
- Fewer courses at upper division levels because of lower enrollments.
- Less opportunity for majors in certain departments to obtain a quality education due to fewer courses.
- Graduates with insufficient background to compete in the marketplace or at graduate schools.
- Alumni become dissatisfied with the undergraduate educational experience in the major.
- Negative feelings spread to others concerning higher education.
- Fewer quality students enter the institution in the department's major.
- Need for fewer faculty in the department.
- More dissatisfaction and frustration among faculty.

Not uncommon in a union setting, especially after retrenchment has taken place, is a faculty reluctance to trust the administration. Administrators, then, not having faculty cooperation, tend to blame the troubles of the entire institution on the faculty. The truth is that the system belongs to the administration (Deming, p. 134). Therefore, to solve problems in such an environment, management must improve faculty and staff morale. These changes cannot take place unless there is collegiality, and unless the administration is committed to providing the facilities, equipment and materials, faculty and improved systems and procedures necessary to meet the demands of the changing environment.

Collegiality, according to Giamatti (1988, p. 39), "*is the shared sense of a shared set of values, values about open access to information, about open exchange of ideas, about academic freedom, about openness of communication and caring; collegiality is the shared belief, regardless of field or discipline, in a generalized, coherent, communal set of attitudes that are collaborative and intellectual. It does not imply unanimity of opinion; it implies commonality of assumption. Collegiality is the most precious asset in any institution of learning, and it is precious to the extent to which it is, if not unspoken, at least unwritten. At its worst, collegiality is a kind of clubbiness, an impulse to exclusivity; at its best, it is a genuinely vital sense of community.*" Collegiality is necessary to successfully introduce the administrative philosophy of Deming to institutions of higher education, especially if Deming's point 11 is to be fully implemented.

Giamatti (pp. 41-42) further notes: "*You will find universities that 10 years ago were run in a collegial fashion now completely structured to look from the outside as if they were manufacturing or banking firms, with tables of organization replete with executive vice-presidents, vice presidents, lawyers: all the appurtenances of a major corporation. ... And when you add to the new corporate management structure the traditional academic distrust of the corporate world, then you have a very interesting situation: the reawakened mistrust of the corporation in the academy occurs in the academy that has now begun to look like a corporation.*"

Administrators must improve the system to provide better educational experiences for students. Administrators must recognize new programs and services necessary to keep the institution at the leading edge for serving the communities. To accomplish these goals, administrators must work closely with the faculty. To do this, administrators and faculty should eliminate adversarial relationships and establish meaningful collegiality.

Chapter 12:
Abolish annual ratings

Administrators should not consider faculty, staff and students as commodities. At all costs, they should remove barriers to pride of workmanship and establish a process permitting recognition for a job well done.

To establish such a process, administrators should prepare an annual Professional Work Plan Agreement (PWPA) with each faculty member. Each PWPA should indicate courses to be taught, what research/creative activities to be conducted and community, school, department and university services to be performed by faculty members to improve the quality of the institution and assist it in meeting its long-range plans. In addition, the PWPA should spell out faculty member personal development goals and what the institution will do to help individuals reach their personal development goals. The evaluation process should also be spelled out in the PWPA. The results of the evaluation should be linked directly to a professional and personal development process; not to a dismissal and/or fear procedure.

According to Deming (p. 103), *"traditional appraisal systems increase the variability of performance of people. The trouble lies in the implied preciseness of rating schemes. What happens is this. Somebody is rated below average, takes a look at people that are rated above average; naturally wonders why the difference exists. He tries to emulate people above average. The result is impairment of performance."*

The following are examples appropriate to the university setting:

Example one. The president, in conjunction with the governing board and the vice president for academic affairs, may decide that for political purposes, a certain enrollment must be obtained for a given academic year. Such a decision may be based upon a statewide resource allocation formula. This goal may, in fact, be part of the institution's long-range plan. In any event, the recruiting and admissions officers will now be evaluated according to the quota.

In many institutions, admission is based neither upon the quality of students nor upon a given program's ability to absorb an increased number of students. Increasing the number of students in the popular programs may result in larger class sizes and too many majors to advise. Other supporting courses will also probably have larger class sizes. In most institutions, incoming students will have neither a proper orientation course nor an extensive assessment. Students will most likely have to be assigned to classes for which their learning styles are ill-suited. The larger classes will result in less discussion and more testing by multiple choice and similar mechanisms. These, coupled with a lower quality of faculty advisement, can result in unsatisfactory educational experiences and a higher number of dropouts.

The recruiting and admissions officers might ask why the university continues this cycle. Why do 30-50 percent of students entering the university drop out? The reason is simple: poorly prepared students, ill-suited for higher education, are recruited and admitted. As a result, a high percentage drop out. Therefore, the recruiting and admissions officers have to work harder to increase enrollments, since they have to bring in additional students to replace those who left (See Figure 8).

The situation is further exacerbated in that the additional students will use equipment, supplies and facilities designed for fewer people. This results in increased wear and breakdown of equipment, which frustrate students and faculty. As a result, faculty and administration are deprived of their right to pride of workmanship.

Evaluating the performance of recruiting and admissions officers by quotas is *"degeneration to counting ... One of the main effects of evaluation of performance is nourishment of short-term thinking and short-time performance. A (person) must have something to show. His superior is forced into numerics. It is easy to count. Counts relieve management of the necessity to contrive a measure with meaning"* (Deming, p. 105).

The aforementioned can be avoided if the administration (president, vice president for academic affairs, vice president of administration and finance, and the deans) work with department chairpersons, the director of student services, the facilities coordinator and the director of the maintenance department in implementing the institutional long-range plan.

Example two. In evaluating faculty, criteria related to scholarly growth is not

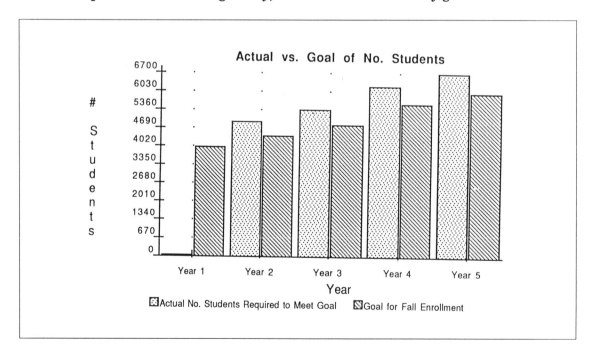

Figure 8: The number of students that might have to reach a quota if a dropout rate of 25 percent occurs for the first two years. The actual number required for admittance might very well be higher if the resources of the institution are inadequate to handle the influx.

86

uncommon. In many institutions, publications and professional presentations are among the primary criteria for successfully demonstrating scholarly growth. We agree with Deming (p. 105) that people measured by counting are deprived of their pride for workmanship. For example, the *"number of designs* (published papers, invited presentations) *that an engineer* (faculty member) *turns out in a period of time would be an example of an index that provides no chance for pride of workmanship. He dare not take time to study and amend the design just completed. To do so would decrease his output."*

A good rating for work on a new program, course, instructional delivery method, testing procedure or assessment project that may generate a better quality graduate five to 10 years hence *"requires enlightened management."* According to Deming (p. 106), someone who *"engages in such work would study changes in education, changes in style of living, migration in and out of urban areas. He would attend meetings of the American Sociological Society, the business section of the American Statistical Association, the American Marketing Association. He would write professional papers to deliver at such meetings, all of which are necessary for the planning of product and service of the future. He would not for years have anything to show for his labors. Meanwhile, in the absence of enlightened management, other people getting good ratings on short-term projects would leave him behind."*

In most institutions, before applying for tenure, faculty members undergo annual evaluations. Sometimes teaching performance is evaluated by peers, who visit the classroom for part of a class or two. The departmental evaluation committee may also consider poorly defined student evaluation data and course syllabi before completing a checklist of items indicating either a "satisfactory" or a "non-satisfactory" ranking. On rare occasions, the committee may add a paragraph, usually praising the faculty member. The chairperson does essentially the same thing. The department evaluation committee and the chairperson also evaluate the faculty member's performance in research/creative activities and service. The latter information is usually supplied to the committee and the chairperson in the form of a portfolio. The dean, having this input, also attempts to evaluate the faculty member. Eventually, these useless evaluations end up on the president's desk. Usually at the end of five years the faculty member is tenured and evaluated every five years thereafter.

Quehl (1988, p. 21) stated: *"Most of the 700,000 faculty are primarily teachers, very many of whom are outstanding. Some faculty — far fewer than we are asked to believe — are truly outstanding scholars and researchers; some scholars are also excellent teachers; many are not."*

It is generally acknowledged that most of the faculty are concerned about how they will be evaluated for promotion and tenure. They believe the main issue for promotion and tenure is based upon the amount of research they accomplish during their first five years of employment. If personnel evaluations established a long-term outlook on research projects as they related to the mission of the institution, universities could possibly take advantage of the excellence in teaching as professors slowly and methodically instituted creative activities.

Quehl (p. 22) notes *"at some institutions, faculty use words like 'pressure-cooker' and 'exhausting' to describe their professional lives. Many faculty fear burnout, and some question the value of their life's work."* If faculty assessment were directly tied to evaluating the system in which they work and to a professional development plan, many of these fears would be removed and pride in workmanship would occur. With the present evaluation systems at most universities and colleges, faculty are afraid to "fail," to experiment, to change. As a result, they continue to do the same old things in the same old ways because they desire to please the administration to get promoted. Lack of leadership among upper level administrators causes this "fear." Staff evaluations, for all practical purposes, end after the sixth-month probationary period.

Such a system is poorly constructed! *"It ... rewards people that do well in the system. It does not reward attempts to improve the system"* (Deming, p. 102).

Attempts to improve the evaluation procedure of managing by objectives ... *"nourishes short-term performance, builds fear, demolishes teamwork, nourishes rivalry and politics. It leaves people bitter, crushed, bruised, battered, desolate, dejected, feeling inferior, some even depressed ..."* (Deming, p. 102). The attempt to measure people's ability with an imprecise procedure results in the loss to the university of constructive relationships and effective management.

Evaluation procedures in most universities, as in other industries, stifle teamwork since the procedures make it difficult for people to work together for the good of the institution (Deming, p. 107). It may be possible to measure individual performances within the purchasing department; however, these evaluations will contribute nothing if they're not somehow tied into the overall goals of the university.

Management and faculty need to establish an evaluation mechanism that includes standards on how employees may fit into the system to deliver a superior educational performance with fairness of judgements. To accomplish this, everyone must plan for the future and encourage teamwork.

Universities will shortly have two groups of faculty: The newly hired who replace faculty that retire or have been employed because of growth, and tenured faculty in their 50s and 60s. Both groups will require an appropriate evaluation of how they fit into the institution and how the institution can provide appropriate professional development to ensure that the institution's long-range plan is on target.

Most new faculty will likely be younger than is traditional since most approved positions are at the assistant professor level. Both administration and faculty will be responsible for evaluating and mentoring the new faculty so they increase their teaching, research and service skills. Older faculty members, many of whom may stay and teach well into the new century, will probably require different incentives for continued growth.

The present evaluation systems used in most colleges and universities don't take advantage of incentives for continued growth since they do not provide appropriate feedback for professional development. In fact, present evaluation systems may act as a threat to the faculty. Worst of all, most current evaluation systems do not fully use the extraordinary expertise of the older faculty.

Clearly, pressure from a number of sources demands that the quality of instruction be upgraded in academic institutions. Parents, legislators and students are concerned about the cost of higher education, and often try to relate this concern to some formula as to why colleges and universities aren't more efficient. Truthfully, this is the fault of administrators, who haven't informed the public about the effectiveness of higher education, how well professors are performing and where and why mistakes were made.

There is no single "best" way to evaluate the faculty — including their teaching, research and service activities. Each tool and/or procedure is limited. However, a variety of mechanisms can provide a balanced set of information for making decisions concerning personnel and how they help fulfill the institution's mission.

We recommend a procedure that initially assesses the teaching style of each faculty member. The results would be on file in the library. Then the learning styles of students would be determined as they enter into the college or university. Students would be assigned, to the extent possible, to classes in which their learning styles match the instructors' teaching styles. If a match isn't possible, students and instructors should be counseled as to possible conflicts.

Then, all classes of every instructor should be evaluated, looking at the following:
- Student evaluation of instruction.
- Student evaluation of the course (apart from instruction).
- Faculty evaluation of students.
- Faculty evaluation of the course.
- Self-evaluation.
- Peer evaluation.

To remove the fear factor, the results of the evaluations should be linked directly to a professional development process that considers that over 70 percent of colleges use student evaluations of instruction. Both students and faculty use and endorse such evaluations. Two of the most frequently used instruments are the Educational Testing Service Student Instructional Report and the Instructional Development and Effectiveness Assessment System from Kansas State University.

Many studies indicate student ratings are reliable, provided enough students have made the ratings. For example, it's much better to have at least 15 students evaluate the professor in as many as 10 courses for effective results. The following factors may influence the ratings:
- **Class size:** Classes with fewer than 10 students are rated best, followed by those with 15 to 35. Classes from 35 to 100 students rated the lowest. Apparently in the smaller classes, instructors were able to adjust the material to fit the students more closely than in larger classes. Classes with more than 35 students may not be conducive to meaningful interaction between students and faculty members.
- **Course Requirement:** Higher ratings are given to courses in the students' majors.
- **Expected Grade:** There is little or no correlation in the overall rating between the grades students anticipate receiving and grades they actually receive.
- **Teacher Characteristics:** Research indicates professors with more teaching experience do better in student ratings than new faculty, especially first year faculty members. However, a slight decline in rated effectiveness during the later years of a teaching career has implications for professional development.
- **Teaching Load:** There is no correlation between teaching load and student ratings. In fact, some studies suggest that a credit hour load of more than 13 resulted in better student evaluations.
- **Research Productivity:** There is no association between research productivity and student ratings.

- **Entertainment vs. Substance:** Highly rated professors are substance teachers; however, teaching of substance and entertainment overlap.
- **Alumni vs. Student Evaluations:** Student and alumni ratings generally agree, so there is no reason to include the latter in the evaluation of faculty.

A standard student evaluation form should be administered during the last two weeks of class. It shouldn't be long, and professors should have the right to add questions of their own. Most importantly, no student evaluation of instruction should be considered for personnel evaluations until five or more courses with 10 to 15 students or more have been evaluated.

Student course evaluations can give valuable information to the instructor and administration about items influencing course quality, such as the course outline, reading materials, the conditions under which, as well as the manner in which, content is delivered.)

Faculty evaluation of students is important since students differ in intelligence, learning attitudes, study habits and commitments, depending upon their maturity, major, etc.

Faculty evaluation of the course can help assess the classroom environment, i.e., how conducive was the learning atmosphere?

Self-evaluation is important in developing an individual's Professional Work Plan Agreement, since it provides the instructor, chairperson and the dean an opportunity to ascertain needed professional development activities. Combined with other evaluation procedures, such as videotaping, self evaluation can be particularly useful in situations where fear has been driven out (Centra 1979).

Peer evaluations are not generally reliable for making tenure, promotion or salary decisions (Centra 1979). However, trained faculty evaluators can make sounder judgements, and it might be wise to have a "center" consisting of trained faculty evaluators who might use videotaped classes, along with other evaluation results, to make specific recommendations to help faculty reach their full potential.

Centra made a good point when he stated: *"Determining the effectiveness of people in their job is far from a perfect science, and it will never be, but by understanding the strengths and limitations of different methods of assessment and applying them equitably, faculty members and administrators will be better able to make fairer decisions ..."*

The results of the annual Professional Work Plan Agreement should be examined yearly, but in light of five-year accomplishments towards the goals of the institution, school, academic department and faculty members. At the same time, academic systems should be examined critically. Trends should begin to establish themselves over a five-year period, not only for employees, but for the system as well. For example, a new course, say a telecourse, may have low enrollments for the first couple of years, and the instructor may receive poor student evaluations. However, in years three to five, after the course is modified and finely tuned, enrollments and student evaluations may improve significantly, especially if student\teacher learning\teaching styles are matched, and if the instructor had a good mentor.

If performance is consistently poor over five years, the person needs help. He/she should be referred to a mentor or a professional development committee where a team effort could help the person fit into the system, determine why the person can't fit in or how the system may be modified. Such a procedure should encourage teamwork rather than allowing the employee to influence a committee or administration.

This point may be the most difficult to introduce into a university that is part of a unionized system. Administration, however, should attempt to follow the steps suggested by Deming as we have modified and elaborated upon them:

- Institute education in the principles and methods of leadership to all employees using the Deming method.
- Carefully select all employees.
- Constantly improve the professional and personal development of all employees.
- Conduct regular teaming seminars.
- Recognize those over the upper control limits of the system and help those below the lower control limits.
- Administrators should hold an annual one-hour interview with their department chairpersons and the dean to review the PWPA.
- Institute an evaluation procedure, like the one described above.
- Discuss data on faculty performance at administrative meetings to help employees improve the system.

The aforementioned effort is known as management by policy deployment (John E. Newcomb 1989, personal communication), and differs from "Management by Objectives" (MBO). According to Newcomb, *"Policy deployment helps to create cohesiveness within an organization by charting a course that's understood throughout the organization. It brings into focus a vision of the future for the organization. The purpose for which an organization exists is defined. The values or principles of the organization support the purposes for which the organization is in business. The values are understood and accepted. Policy deployment provides a structure with which to identify clear organizational objectives. It integrates and orchestrates the efforts of all within an organization into actions which move the entire organization toward its objectives. Objectives are targets for improvement against which we can measure progress."*

Management by policy deployment, therefore, provides the backbone which permits individuals to realize their potential and contribution, and brings the long-term vision into focus. Policy deployment draws the entire university together toward appropriate changes necessary to attain long-term vision. As a result, morale will increase since people will be able to see how their contributions add to the values and vision of those practiced and preached by the institution.

Much of the lack of progress in educational institutions results from the seeming unwillingness of faculty to change. When a change in attitude does not occur, behavior doesn't change and neither do results. With new systems introduced with management by policy deployment, the institution can break the cycle represented in figures one and two.

Deming (p. 173) makes the following remarks about the quality of teaching: *"How do you define quality of teaching? How do you define a good teacher? I offer comment only in respect to higher education. The first requisite for a good teacher is that he have something to teach. His aim should be to give inspiration and direction to students for further study. To do this, a teacher must possess knowledge of the subject. The only operational definition of knowledge requisite for teaching is research. Research need not be earthshaking. It may only be a new derivation of knowledge or principles already established. Publication of original research in reputable journals is an index of achievement. This is an imperfect measure, but none better has been found.*

"In my experience, I have seen a teacher hold 150 students spellbound, teaching what is wrong. His students rated him as a great teacher. In contrast, two of my own greatest teachers in universities would be rated poor teachers on every count. Then why did people come from all over the world to study with them, including me? For the simple reason that these men had something to teach. They inspired their students to carry on further research. They were leaders of thought — by name, Sir Ronald Fisher in statistics at University College, and Sir Ernest Brown in lunar theory at Yale. Their works will remain classic for centuries. Their students had a chance to observe what these great men were thinking about, and how they built roads into new knowledge."

Chapter 13:
Education and self-improvement

Traditional education delivered in a prescribed way was once the accepted way, but concerns in recent years about cost and educational competency have brought new emphasis to quality of education. Consequently, consumers are demanding a higher quality of education at the best cost.

One way to assure the quality of education is through instituting a vigorous program of education and self-improvement for employees. Deming (p. 86) states: *"What an organization needs is not just good people; it needs people that are improving with education."*

Administrators can no longer delegate the responsibility of continuing education to individuals or committees. The administration must demonstrate leadership for constant quality improvement by challenging others to develop programs of education and mentoring for self-improvement. Until now it's been convenient for schools to have passive faculty development committees, which have traditionally provided little faculty and staff guidance.

In the university of the future, demands will be toward total commitment to educating faculty and staff so consumers receive the highest quality education possible. For colleges and universities to assure themselves that everyone will be part of a vigorous program of education and self-improvement, they should establish professional and personal development committees for both faculty and staff. Each committee should identify the continuing education needs of the constituency and should receive funds to implement their recommendations.

Professional and personal development committees should support educational endeavors that permit those who attend educational activities to teach others to improve the system. The administration must realize, however, that a professional and personal development committee cannot guarantee that the faculty and staff have the education and/or the opportunity for education, self-improvement and mentoring. The committee is just one way of bolstering the self-improvement process. This is very important — each institution should have a full-time director for human potential development, who should report directly to the president.

Administrative units should identify weaknesses common to most faculty and/or staff, and employ consultants to conduct workshops and seminars to improve human competencies and the system. For help in meeting this challenge, leaders in higher education should look to local industries in which competency, competition and pressures have already forced them to deal with the "quality" issue. These businesses will most likely have consultants who will gladly conduct workshops and seminars designed to increase competencies and quality to improve the "system." In addition, businesses can supply mentors to upper-level students to encourage them to develop their skills.

Deming says quality begins and ends with education, and that learning need not be connected with a person's job to be valuable to the employer (Walton 1986). The idea is to keep people's minds functioning and prevent stagnation.

Administrators should realize the half-life of scientific knowledge is approximately two and one-half years. That is, one-half of scientific knowledge is obsolete or changed within two and one-half years. Continuing education, therefore, is a must if administrators expect the science faculty to be good teachers and researchers.

Instituting vigorous programs for education, self-improvement and mentoring also increases morale, which should result in a better system: better faculty, better support staff, better instruction, and, as a result, better graduates. Personnel evaluation, especially faculty, should be directly linked to a program for professional development. In chapter 12, we mentioned some of the limitations of faculty evaluations. Most evaluation procedures have problems, including dishonest peer evaluations, and evaluations conducted by people not educated in the process who are most likely using instruments ill-suited for the task (Centra 1979). Only when proper evaluations are conducted, weaknesses are recognized, teamwork is encouraged and fear is removed from the system, will education, self-improvement and mentoring programs be successful.

The purpose of education, self-improvement and mentoring, therefore, is to improve one's competency and worth to the organization, because individuals who stop learning become stagnant. The administration must be constantly aware that the world is in a continual state of change; hence knowledge becomes outdated very rapidly, especially in the sciences. A planned program, therefore, must be implemented which will improve the academic backgrounds of individuals in their specific fields of knowledge. This can be accomplished through workshops, seminars and conferences that broaden the concepts associated with specific fields of knowledge.

Management in universities and colleges must take a new look at their obligation to implement a planned program for education, self-improvement and mentoring for faculty and staff. Education can be meaningful only if the teaching staff is current, knowledgeable and professionally competent. Continuing education is essential to maintain and improve educational programs and classroom instruction. The failure to keep professors current can only introduce chaos into the system.

Institutions of higher education must require good teaching and appropriate resources for knowledge transmission and retrieval. Therefore, content and skills necessary for the faculty to understand and use new techniques and knowledge must be available to them. If they do not know the purpose or have the necessary skills to use these resources, faculty and staff will not be able to improve. Management is obliged, therefore, to suffuse planned continuing education and self improvement throughout the organization.

Of the many ways to institute self-improvement programs, we suggest only a few. Common to all programs is the underlying assumption that classroom instruction can be improved. This implies the instructor's behavior in the classroom will change. For this to occur, managers must plan improvement programs for professional development geared toward behavioral change that will lead to more effective teacher-pupil interaction.

Involve educators in planning

It is imperative, therefore, that individuals affected by continuing education activities be involved in the planning process. In most meetings in universities, the 80/20 rule takes effect: 80 percent of the talking is done by 20 percent of the people, and the 20 percent doing the talking are most likely those with the highest rank, i.e. presidents, provosts, vice presidents, deans, chairpersons, etc. In reality, however, the most prominent function of a college or university is teaching, and this is done by the faculty. Faculty members know many of the problems and may have suggestions for resolving them, but those who control the resources and the system have to listen and become informed.

An administrator's style can have a tremendous effect upon professional growth. For example, an autocratic style can have a deadly effect, and may not encourage diversity and innovation. As a result, people wanting to get a positive rating from their managers will conform to the traditional or expected way. Deming believes this style of leadership only creates fear and stifles creativity.

On the other hand, administrators who encourage professional growth activities but who don't take the advice of those involved in the activities, will soon learn that surface compliance will occur but there will be little change in behavior. Inertia sets in. The Deming philosophy stresses the need for employees to be involved in the planning process. Deming states that anyone who has brought his work to a state of status quo, whether trained well or not, is in a rut. The person needs new training (p. 249). How well this applies to higher education!

In most settings, secretaries for given academic departments will neither know nor appreciate the complexities of financial aid, student affairs, payroll, finance, etc. However, annual in-house workshops dealing with the functions and procedures of all facets of the university would encourage teaming among all secretaries.

Since faculty and staff attend a variety of professional meetings, would it not be advantageous upon their return to present seminars or written reports to other units within the academy? Why do universities let the expertise of their own faculty and staff fade into the file cabinets? When will all universities hire a director for human potential development? When this occurs, a true "Aquarian Conspiracy" will have begun (Ferguson 1980), and if the person reported directly to the president, the gong for quality would surely be rung.

In the School of Science, Management and Technologies (SM&T) at Edinboro University of Pennsylvania (EUP), we began to implement education and self-improvement as follows:

- We allocated travel funds directly to each academic department so the faculty and chairperson could determine how the money would be distributed. To show the importance of this allocation, department chairpersons had to provide an annual written report about the professional development programs their faculty attended.
- A faculty and staff professional and personal development committee was formed to determine activities requiring funding that would cut across disciplines. The committee was allocated funds to support these

educational endeavors, and the faculty receiving support were expected to present seminars for the entire school/university.

- Monthly meetings for secretaries were held to determine what workshops and/or training they desired to continue to increase the quality of their work. Interestingly, secretaries requested and were sent to a workshop on "How to Deal with Difficult People." Since then the secretaries have initiated a support group, which has greatly increased their morale.
- In the school's long-range plan, the chairs included action activities indicating they would publish and submit grant proposals to be role models for the rest of the faculty.
- Chairpersons and their secretaries requested informational activities from non-academic units of the university to better understand their functions.
- A luncheon seminar series was instituted for secretaries who were interested in expanding their horizons and increasing their efficiency and quality of work. Furthermore, they were given information to enable them to become administrative assistants should such opportunities occur.
- To stress the importance of the professional development activities, the dean required a brief written report from each participant attending a function.

For the university as a whole, we suggested in-house workshops designed to initiate a system of quality improvement. These workshops would include teams from administration, faculty, secretarial staff, union leaders, support services and maintenance. Each workshop would be designed so individuals from each department could meet to identify problems, gather data and eventually solve problems as a team. These workshops, following W. Edward Deming's recommendations for transformation management and quality control, would culminate in a written and oral report of their efforts.

Specific objectives for the teaming workshop follow:

- To help the university improve quality, productivity and competitive positioning.
- To promote interaction and better communication between service areas to identify and solve problems quickly and more efficiently.
- To introduce Deming's management principles, statistical quality control and continuous improvement strategies to advance the quality of instruction.
- To provide an opportunity for feedback on projects and to interact with service organizations performing similar quality transformation projects.

Chapter 14:
Involve everyone in the transformation

As Deming noted (p. 86), institutions will struggle over each of the first thirteen points before his philosophy can be instituted. Implementing this management style in any institution can cause great concerns, however, the rewards are sufficiently great to justify the effort.

To accomplish the transformation the administration should explain through seminars and other methods how the administrative system will involve everybody, every job, every activity and every process. Leaders should also move at a deliberate speed to guide the institution toward continual improvement of quality.

Deming developed a model of continual improvement (p. 180) that's shown in the following figure:

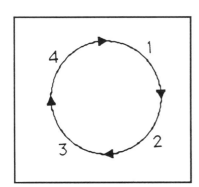

In the above figure, the four segments (p. 181) represent the following:
1. Design the product.
2. Make it; test it in the production line and the laboratory.
3. Put it on the market.
4. Test it in service; find out what users think of it and why non-users haven't bought it.

The circular process never ends. The steps are repeated in an endless cycle of improvement. As applied to the development of a curriculum these steps might become:

1. Design a curriculum to meet a perceived need.
2. Develop methods to test components of the curriculum before the curriculum is fully implemented.
3. Implement the curriculum.
4. Evaluate the results by assessing student achievement and employer satisfaction.

Step four leads back to step one, where the curriculum is updated and the cycle continues. Because of its open-ended cyclical nature, the process might better be referred to as a helical process to emphasize its ongoing nature. This is illustrated in the following figure (p.98).

The major point of the figure above is that there's no end to the process. Satisfaction is never achieved. The next turn around the spiral always waits.

Everyone must be involved in efforts to achieve constantly improving quality. Within each subsystem of the institution, the helical model must be applied as appropriate. Each step in the helix is critical and must be fully understood to be implemented. Too often, institutions follow only the first three steps in the helical

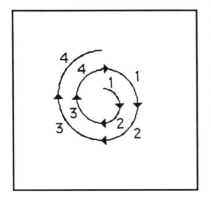

model. Systems are put into place but never evaluated, which can lead to serious dislocations within the institution.

One example of a serious dislocation tells how it took over eight months for a computer equipment order to be filled. It illustrates how a poorly designed system, which violates a number of Deming's points, can cause frustration.

The following people/departments were involved: Provost/vice president for academic affairs, a dean, four department chairpersons, a vice president for computing services, a vice president for administration, a purchasing agent and four members of the computer center. All were most likely given excellent annual evaluations within their subsystems, until one member pointed out the inefficiency within the system: the computer order was delayed. The study shows how various people within the "subsystems" reacted to the inefficiency. Several people felt that pointing out the inefficiency would threaten their performance evaluation. Thus the practice of performance review was inhibiting improvement in the system. It was deemed prudent simply to refuse to admit a problem existed until one individual exposed it.

Order the damn computers, please

Day one: An academic dean is informed by the vice president for academic affairs (VPAA) that his school has been allocated funds for equipment. The dean meets with the department chairpersons, and all agree that a certain brand of computers should be purchased (the school's long-range plan indicates this is a top priority).

Day two: The dean submits the purchase order to the office of the director of finance where it remains for 35 days.

Day 37: The dean inquires about the order. The director of finance only now forwards it to the vice president for computing services, as such an order requires his approval.

Day 43: The vice president for computing services calls the dean to ask what the computers are for. The vice president for computing services then forwards his recommendation to the vice president for administration as the order requires yet another approval. The recommendation is that this particular brand of computer not be purchased and that another brand be substituted. This information is not relayed to the dean. The vice president for administration delays the process for another 30 days and does not inform the dean.

Day 73: The vice president for administration, who has no computer background, informs the VPAA that the computer order is not appropriate.

Day 77: The VPAA informs the dean via telephone that the computer order was not submitted because it was not appropriate, but gives no specific reasons.

Day 78: The dean invites the computer center staff to the facilities for which the computers were to be used. The staff agrees the original order was appropriate for the school.

Day 82: The dean informs the vice president for administration of the error and describes the fiasco as of that date. The vice president for administration threatens the dean with presidential reprisal if the vice president's office is reflected upon poorly.

Day 100: The original computer order is now approved by the vice president for computing services and the vice president for administration, and the order is placed. However, prices have increased 15 percent and the computers are now on back order.

Day 210: The equipment that was originally recommended for substitution by the vice president for computer services is discontinued.

Day 240: The computers arrive.

The key to getting everyone involved in the transformation is to change the emphasis from individual performance reviews (such as those cited above) to systems evaluations. When the emphasis is on personal performance reviews, problems become identified with a particular individual's failure to perform. Of course, no one wishes to admit to personal failure, so problems are denied or ignored. With systems review, the problem is with the *system*, not the individual. Thus, identifying a problem is not personally threatening to anyone. In fact, identifying a problem and finding a solution become activities that merit praise. The idea is to turn each improvement in the system into a cause for group celebration. This encourages further improvement by all group members and removes fear of exposing system weaknesses.

Since the student is the outgoing product, and since human beings cannot and should not be molded into a commodity, deviations will occur with graduates. Employers, however, should not be expected to "rework," i.e. educate employees in the beginning skills that should have already been obtained. Unfortunately, American employers have come to expect the products of our educational system to be incomplete, and as a result, they've become accustomed to reworking (re-educating) the products (graduates). The reasons are clear: Most institutions of higher education neither provide the expected terminal competencies to graduates, nor do employers expect graduates to have these skills. Both industry and academic institutions must unite in a common crusade for quality. This crusade, however, must be driven, even forcefully, into the very beginnings of our system — elementary schools via teacher education programs. When our society remunerates our K-12 teachers at least twice the amount of the sanitary workers in our large cities, perhaps our universities will pressure professors to permit only qualified students to graduate. With regard to politicians, Giamatti (p. 96) wrote: *"If a society assumes its politicians are venal, stupid or self-serving, it will attract to its public life as an ongoing self-fulfilling prophecy the greedy, the knavish and the dim."* The same exact point can be made with teachers — until society gives proper recognition to teachers, the better talent will enter other fields.

The public has not recognized the price of poorly paid teachers and is just as responsible as university administrators and industry CEOs for the deterioration of the gray matter within our society. There is no innate immunity from this disease. Improvement can occur only when our university administrators create a constancy of purpose toward continuous improvement, including the K-12 education they indirectly control, since they educate the teachers and administrators. After all, *"when we ask what shall be done about our public schools, we are asking what shall be done about the future of our country"* (Giamatti 1988, p. 71). A major cause of problems in our society might very well lie in the leadership within our universities.

Giamatti (pp. 60-61) makes the following statement about our public schools:"*Beneath the layers of anxiety that our schools are riddled with truancy, absenteeism, dropping out and violence; that all the standard measures indicate a decline in the national ability to read and write and reckon; that teachers have lost their dedication and students their motivation and the whole system its quality; is the deepest anxiety: that no one is paying attention. The fear that local political leaders do nothing to assert the critical priority of local schools, that national leaders retreat to bureaucratic bunkers or simply fail to acknowledge the plight of schools, terrifies the people, particularly when the people know in their blood that somehow schools and education are still linked to jobs, economic growth and productivity, and a decent public order. The people believe those linkages but hear nothing about them from public officials, elected or appointed. And so the confusion grows until it is not hysterical but necessary to ask, What will happen to all young Americans' access to the American educational dream if the public schools fail or falter?*"

Most shortcomings of our public school systems can be blamed directly on the lack of leadership in higher education, and unless it is corrected, private education will have to respond to keep America from slipping too far behind in the world economy. But if college administrators got everyone involved in the transformation to quality education, faculty would work closely with the public, including people from industry and government, and many deficiencies in our school systems would be corrected.

If academic institutions are to adopt a new quality philosophy, administrators must pledge they will not be intimidated into graduating anyone who has not met expected competencies. Administrations must not only drive the "idea" of quality into employees, they must also insist that quality standards be implemented.

Change is in the air. Can institutions of higher education afford *not* to incorporate Deming's principles into an administrative philosophy?

Case Studies

This section addresses actual events that have taken place at a variety of universities. Although names and titles have been changed to save embarrassment, the events point out "system" errors that could have been avoided had Deming's principles been applied successfully.

Case Study one: In case of inclement weather, don't tell the chairpersons

A directive from the dean's office explicitly stated who would contact whom in case the university had to be closed due to inclement weather. It was clear from the dean's memo that upon receiving orders from the president, the provost/vice president for academic affairs would contact the academic deans. The dean of one unit indicated he would contact the civil service personnel and that the chairpersons were to contact their respective faculty, but no one had the responsibility of contacting the chairpersons. Perhaps chairpersons are supposed to be clairvoyant?

Confusion could have been avoided if the dean or his staff had carefully examined the memorandum before distribution.

Point violated:

Number five: Improve constantly and forever the system of production and service to improve quality and productivity.

Case Study two: Space allocation — no problem

The following memo was sent by the newly hired director of a new school to the executive vice president:

I was employed as the director of professional school on 1 May, 1982. My notes indicate the following communications regarding space.

May 6, 1982. I met with you to indicate the space that would be required to implement the newly approved programs. You indicated that these needs were being addressed and that you would get back to me in the very near future.

June 23, 1982. I discussed the space problems with you, as new faculty were being hired to implement the programs in September of 1983. You indicated that you would look into the matter and see what was holding up the action.

August 2, 1982. The space and equipment needs were forwarded to you so that we could have these on hand by September of next year.

August 31, 1982. Please find attached a memo indicating agenda item "space" which was discussed on September 3, 1980 at the academic council meeting.

November 5, 1982. Please find attached a memo from the associate vice president for resource allocation, which identified the space that could be allocated to the professional school.

November 22, 1982. Notes from a meeting with you indicate that the professional school will have the necessary equipment, space and faculty necessary for us to accept students.

January 4, 1983. I met with you from 3 to 4 p.m. You indicated that I should meet with the associate vice president for resource allocation next week to iron out the final details for space. You also indicated that you were making the necessary budget transfer for us to finally submit our equipment request.

March 31, 1983. The programs in the school made a declaration of intent to apply for accreditation in which we projected the space that would be allocated. Please note that I indicated that one of the site visits will occur on November 18, 1983; however, there was no correlation between the proposed space and budget allocation and the actual allocations which are yet to be made.

April 26, 1983. James Lovit (assistant director) and I met with you to discuss projected space needs.

May 9, 1983. I gave you a "draft" of a letter rescinding the admission of students, if the space and equipment were not on hand by July. You assured us (assistant director and chairpersons) that the equipment and laboratories would be in place and not to worry.

May 19, 1983. I again asked about the space and equipment.

July 5, 1983. You indicated to me that the laboratory space would not be available in time for the fall admissions.

My chairpersons and I met with you on July 12, July 29, August 30, September 12, September 14, September 23, September 28 and finally on September 29, 1983. At this point I asked the university's legal counsel for advice on terminating our students as we will not be able to teach or get accreditation. I requested at that time that we meet with the president to discuss this matter.

(As of May 1, 1984 neither the space requirement nor the equipment allocation was forthcoming. The director resigned!)

Points violated: All!

Case Study three: Faculty development allocation — let her do the work

During the budget-building process or lack thereof, since the procedure was largely a "blue-sky request," each of the academic deans was given explicit directions. Dean A detailed a faculty development plan and justified the large request, whereas deans B and C submitted nominal increases with no justification.

When the allocations were made, each dean received the amount he/she requested. The vice president for academic affairs, however, reclaimed the faculty development money and divided it equally among all the schools. In fact, it was later discovered that the provost and the vice president had both agreed to approve dean A's request, as it was well-done and justified, but they intended to divide the money as they saw fit.

As a result, dean A was penalized for her efficiency. The budget problems could have been avoided if, during the budget-building process, all the deans had submitted requests based on justifiable plans.

Point violated:

Number 11: Eliminate quotas and numerical goals; substitute leadership.

Case Study four: The geographic axis

After a reorganization of the university into four schools, the deans were instructed by the provost/VPAA to work out a geographic axis that would concentrate each school in a given region. The deans were instructed to work among themselves and make recommendations to the provost/VPAA about resource allocations so she could forward the suggestions to a university committee.

For nearly a year the deans met weekly to consider in detail what had to be done to accomplish such a move. The provost/VPAA liked the plan and sent it to the committee on resource allocation. The chairperson of the committee sent the recommendation to the executive assistant to the president, who did not forward the recommendation to the president. However, the provost/VPAA assumed that since the president did not react to the suggestions, all was well and the move was to take place. The deans were instructed to inform the faculty that a switch was to take place in the near future. The deans followed the orders and informed the faculty. (At this point it should be noted that *only* the president and the faculty did not know of the plans.)

As a result, the faculty from four of the departments affected by the move responded with the following memo:

"As chairpersons of these departments, we wish to convey the strong negative feelings and indignation of our colleagues, including ourselves, to such a plan. We would be remiss to do otherwise. To say that the departments are upset is a gross understatement.

"As a group, we are profoundly troubled over the manner in which this plan has evolved. It is only common decency that these and other plans be formally discussed with those faculty members directly affected before this plan becomes a fait accompli."

The next day the president was confronted at a university senate meeting regarding the proposed change in the "Geographic Axis." He answered he did not know what the question was about, as he was unaware of the proposed move.

The provost/vice president for academic affairs and the executive assistant to the president were relieved of their duties shortly thereafter.

This unpleasant situation could have been avoided if the president had first been asked if he approved a geographic axis move and if the faculty that were to be involved had been asked to participate in the decision.

Points Violated:

Number 12: Remove barriers that rob employees of their right to pride in workmanship.

Number 14: Involve everyone in the transformation to quality.

Case Study five: The preregistration process needs improvement

After a fiasco in the preregistration process in which students waited in line for 15 hours only to discover that the courses they needed were not available, the president demanded that the registrar meet with the deans to make sure this did not happen again. (The registrar was reprimanded for her inability to plan and to improve the system.) The registrar called a meeting.

Attending the meeting were the registrar, four academic deans and three assistant deans. After 15 minutes of deliberation it was decided that the present fiasco was caused by the **previous** vice president for academic affairs, and that in the future a sufficient number of courses would be scheduled to handle all anticipated enrollment. In the following 1.5 hours, excuses were given for why in the highly computerized campus, the mainframe computer could not be used for preregistration, checking the graduation list and for other flexible registration procedures.

The meeting would have been productive if it had either been concluded during the first 15 minutes or if the computer center had placed an action-oriented person who would be responsive to the needs of the students on the committee.

How much did such a non-productive meeting cost the institution? How frequently does this kind of waste occur in institutions of higher education? Would it not have been better to admit the mistakes of the present registration process instead of blaming a previous administrator who had little to do with the fiasco? Who will be responsible when a similar fiasco occurs next year?

Point violated:

Number 12: Remove barriers that rob employees of their right to pride in workmanship.

Case Study six: Urgent faculty development

A memo from the office of the vice president for academic affairs dated 7 September to the academic deans: "Our annual faculty development report was due in the system office on September 1. A form to assist you in the record keeping was to be implemented in your offices last summer. We need to know as quickly as possible the number of faculty involved in the specific categories of activities and in unusual or exemplary projects. Please assist us to prepare this important report promptly and return the forms as quickly as possible."

The deans replied: **What forms?**

Needless to say, everyone was running about trying to reconstruct the travel and professional development activities of the faculty over the past year. Perhaps the administration requires professional development to eliminate instances such as these?

Points Violated:

Number nine: Break down barriers between departments.

Number 13: Institute a vigorous program of education and self-improvement.

Case Study seven: Tenure — for your information this is the new policy

The board of governors at a university was concerned about the number of faculty who had obtained tenure. Their concern was based on the fact that this university did not want more than 60 percent of the faculty tenured. Board members were concerned that if more faculty were tenured, perhaps "new blood" wouldn't transfuse the ranks, and the quality of teaching and research would languish. The board requested that the president examine the present tenure policy and modify it to make acquiring tenure more difficult. The president, without any participation from the faculty, modified the policy and then proceeded to inform the faculty senate of the new policy. Needless to say, the faculty were irate, and expressed a no-confidence vote in the president. After a major disruption in faculty morale, teaching and research performance, the public perception of this university declined. The president resigned shortly after rescinding the policy.

Points Violated:

Number nine: Break down barriers between departments.

Number 12: Remove barriers that rob people of their right to pride of workmanship.

Number 14: Involve everyone in the transformation to quality.

Case Study eight: We now have an extension center; however...

A university recently obtained facilities for off-campus instructional use in an urban setting. The facilities were remodeled to provide classrooms. Input was sought from those not directly involved in the instruction, and as a result, after three weeks into the semester, the academic dean sent the vice president of buildings and grounds the following memo:

"The instructors and students are concerned about a number of items with regard to the new facility. If things do not improve within the next several weeks, I believe that we will lose enrollments in our extension center. Please note the following:

- Lights: There are no lights in the parking lot, and the students have to bring their own flashlights. When will the lights be installed?
- Housekeeping: There are no trays for the chalkboards, and the dust is settling over the walls and floors. Whose responsibility is it to clean this facility?
- Windows and heating: The temperature was in the '90s, and the windows could not be opened. When we tried to use the heat pump for cooling purposes, it did not work. The heat pump is also the source for heating the facility, and it is inoperable. What happens when the weather turns cold?
- Bathrooms: The women's bathroom has see-through windows which need to be covered. Paper towels are now available (without dispensers), but there are no waste paper baskets for the dirty towels. Also, the water is rusty because of infrequent use. Is there anything that can be done to clean up the toilet bowels and the bathrooms?
- Chairs: There is a lot of borrowing of chairs back and forth between the two classrooms. Can't we get 15 to 20 folding chairs that can be stored in the third room or in the back hall for this purpose?
- AV equipment: At some point in the near future we must be ready to handle this kind of request.
- Books: After three weeks, a class at the extension center still does not have books. Apparently the book van cannot locate the extension center — please give the driver directions. Thanks."

Most, if not all, of the aforementioned could have been avoided through proper planning by both the managers and those professors who would use the facility. Would it not have been better to delay opening the facility until it was ready? What kind of initial impression did the facility have on its first students?

Points Violated:

Number three: Cease dependency on inspection.

Number seven: Improve leadership.

Number nine: Break down barriers between departments.

Number 12: Remove barriers that rob employees of their right to pride in workmanship.

Number 13: Institute a vigorous program of education and self-improvement.

Number 14: Involve everyone in the transformation to quality.

Case Study nine: Textbook shortage

The following memo was sent to the vice president for academic affairs two days before the beginning of classes in the fall semester:

"I am convinced that the bookstore manager did her best to order the appropriate quantity of books for the classes. However, Ms. Smith has been ordering books from the faculty estimate forms while the dean has been increasing class sizes, and you have added additional sections as late as last week. Doesn't anyone in administration talk to the bookstore manager? Every year at this time we get late-deciders, late-adders and poorly motivated students who then use inability to get access to a text as one of the excuses for dropping out. Then we wonder why we have such poor academic performance and high attrition."

Points Violated:

Number three: Cease dependency on inspection.

Number seven: Improve leadership.

Number nine: Break down barriers between departments.

Number 12: Remove barriers that rob employees of their right to pride in workmanship.

Number 13: Institute a vigorous program of education and self-improvement.

Number 14: Involve everyone in the transformation to quality.

Case Study 10: Urgent — Parents' Day

The vice president for academic affairs receives a reminder from the director of recreation that the annual parents' day is scheduled 15 days hence. Four days before the scheduled event, the deans are asked to provide representatives from their academic departments so name tags can be prepared. The deans are informed that the schedule of events will be delivered that afternoon.

Point violated:

Number 10: Replace slogans, exhortations and targets with methods that work.

Case Study 11: Call the ambulance, please

Sometimes students will panic and call an ambulance for medical assistance when none is needed. There can also be occasional prank calls for an ambulance. To prevent unnecessary ambulance calls, a policy dictated that students could not directly call for ambulance assistance. Instead, they were required to call the campus police, who would make a personal visit to the site of the problem to assess whether an ambulance was really needed.

There were two problems with this policy: a) the police had received no special training to qualify them to make emergency medical decisions, and b) the time lost while the police made a special trip to the emergency site could, in some cases, make the difference between life and death.

The real issue here was one of cost. Dollars would be lost in unnecessary ambulance trips. What suffered was the quality of the service offered (delay in ambulance response time). One major litigation based on the delay in response time would very likely wipe out years of savings realized by saving a few unnecessary ambulance runs.

Point violated:

Number four: Minimize total cost.

Case Study 12: Procedure for hiring new faculty

The process for hiring faculty at this southern university was not as responsive as the vice president for academic affairs would like to have seen it, so he transferred the process to the offices of the academic deans. One dean, upon receiving the hiring responsibility, was notified that the process could not be changed since it was approved by the Affirmative Action/Equal Opportunity Employment (AA/EOE) officer and the other members of the management team, but he was responsible for instituting the process. The dean, after examining the directions, wrote the following memo to his colleagues:

"Colleagues, please inform me if I am wrong, but I believe the following procedure is what we have to follow to hire faculty.

1. The department completes a position request and justification level request for faculty form with appropriate information and supporting documentation.

2. The associate vice president for faculty relations provides a position number for the requested position.

3. The school dean reviews and approves/rejects/modifies the request in consultation with the chairperson of the department and forwards the request to the provost/vice president for academic affairs.

4. The provost/VPAA reviews the request and approves/rejects it or may request additional information. If the position is for a tenured track professor and is approved, the provost/VPAA puts the request on the agenda of the council of deans. If the position is for a temporary, part-time faculty member, the provost/VPAA gives approval and hiring can begin.

5. The council of deans reviews personnel requests and recommends a list for inclusion into the university's personnel plan which occurs twice a year.

6. The provost/VPAA reviews the recommendations from the council of deans and either accepts or rejects requests for positions. The accepted recommendations are refined and forwarded to the Institutional Resource Allocation Committee (IRAC) for consideration. (The IRAC consists of the four vice presidents.) The rejected positions are sent back to the school dean.

7. The IRAC reviews and either approves or rejects the requests for new faculty. The IRAC verifies that the requests comply with the institutional master plan. The rejected requests are returned to the Provost/VPAA. The approved requests are forwarded to the president for consideration and approval.

8. The president considers the requests and either approves or rejects or asks for additional information. The approved requests are forwarded to the provost/VPAA.

9. The provost/VPAA forwards the approved requests to the associate vice president for faculty relations.

10. The associate vice president for faculty relations notifies the appropriate school dean of the approvals to hire.

11. The dean notifies the appropriate department chairperson of the approval(s). The dean and chairperson collaborate to ensure the proper job description, advertisements with deadlines, and qualifications are forwarded to the AA/EOE.

12. The chairperson sets up the appropriate department selection committee.

13. The dean consults with the AA/EOE to ensure guidelines are in order.

14. The dean consults with the provost/VPAA and receives approval for advertising the position.

15. The position is advertised through the dean's office.

16. The dean approves the department selection committee and reviews the list of questions that are to be asked of each candidate. The questions may have to be modified per instructions of dean. The dean forwards the questions to the AA/EOE Officer for approval. Certain questions may be deleted and/or added per suggestion of the AA/EOE Officer.

17. The dean's office receives the applications, acknowledges receipt, sends AA/EOE material and literature about the university to the candidates, and examines the completeness of the applications.

18. The AA/EOE officer reviews the pool of candidates and approves the candidate pool.

19. The applicant pool is forwarded to the chairperson of the selection committee. The committee considers the pool with respect to the advertised guidelines and recommends candidates for interview to the dean.

20. The dean sends the recommended interview pool to the AA/EOE officer for approval. The AA/EOE officer may require additional candidates for interview.

21. The dean informs the selection committee of the approval to interview and the travel expense guidelines.

22. The selection committee notifies the finalists and arranges for the interviews.

23. The selection committee conducts the interviews in accordance with the previously determined questions and guidelines.

24. The selection committee provides recommendation to hire to the department chairperson.

25. The department chairperson calls a department meeting.

26. The entire department votes on the recommended candidate(s).

27. The department chairperson forwards all documents of all candidates with recommendation of what candidate to hire to the dean.

28. The dean prepares a packet containing all search materials, recommendation including rank and salary for consideration by the provost/VPAA. Also included is a draft memo prepared by the dean for the provost/VPAA to the president recommending

appointment. The packet is sent to the president the information is first reviewed by the associate vice president for faculty relations.

29. The associate vice president for faculty relations sends the packet of information to the provost/VPAA.

30. The provost/VPAA reviews all of the material and makes a recommendation to the president. (Rank and salary may be different from what was recommended by the dean and/or chairperson.

31. The president reviews the recommendation. If approved, the dean will be informed and the dean's office will prepare an appointment letter for the president's signature.

32. The president informs the successful candidate in writing.

33. The written acceptance of the successful candidate is received.

34. Rejection letters are sent out by the dean's office to unsuccessful candidates.

35. The dean's office follows up with the successful candidate and forwards schedules and orientation material.

References

Agor, Weston 1984. *Intuitive Management: Integrating Left and Right Brain Management Skills.* Englewood Cliffs, NJ: Prentice Hall.

Bedeian, Arthur G. and Gluek, William F. 1983. *Management.* 3rd ed., Hinsdale, IL: Dryden Press.

Bennis, Warren and Nanus, Burt 1985. *Leaders.* New York: Harper & Row.

Blake, R.R., Mouton, J.S., and Williams, M.S. 1981. *The Academic Administrators Grid.* San Francisco: Jossey-Bass.

Block, Peter 1987. *The Empowered Manager.* San Francisco: Jossey-Bass.

Bradford, David L. and Cohen, Allan R. 1984. *Managing For Excellence.* New York: John Wiley & Sons, Inc.

Broce, T.E. 1979. *Fund Raising: The Guide to Raising Money from Private Sectors.* Norman, OK: University of Oklahoma Press.

Brooks, Glenn 1984. "Aphorisms and Maxims for Chief Academic Officers." In David G. Brown (Ed.), *Leadership Roles of Chief Academic Officers.* San Francisco: Jossey-Bass.

Burns, James MacGregor 1978. *Leadership.* New York: Harper & Row.

Centra, John 1988. *Determining Faculty Effectiveness.* San Francisco: Jossey-Bass.

Claxton, Charles S. and Murrell, Patricia H. 1987. *Learning Styles: Implications for Improving Education Practices.* ASHE-ERIC Higher Education Report No. 4. Washington, DC: Association for the Study of Higher Education.

Cornesky, Robert A. and Anderson, John A. 1987. "Fund-Raising Strategies for the Allied Health Professions." *Journal of Allied Health*, May.

Cornesky, Robert A. and Bolte, John 1986. *Long-Range Planning and Resource Allocation Procedures for Colleges and Universities.* Lubbock: Texas Tech University Center for Professional Development.

Darling, John and Cornesky, Robert A. 1987. "Retrospective Observations of Successful Administrators in Institutions of Higher Education." Unpublished.

Darling, John R. and Cornesky, Robert A. 1987. "Keys to Conflict Management: A Case Study from an Academic Health Sciences Center." *Leadership and Organization Development Journal.*

Deming, W. Edwards 1986. *Out of the Crisis.* Cambridge: Massachusetts Institute of Technology Center for Advanced Engineering Study.

Dessler, Gary 1986. *Organizational Theory.* 2d ed. Englewood Cliffs, NJ: Prentice-Hall.

Dressel, Paul L. 1981. *Administrative Leadership.* San Francisco: Jossey-Bass.

Drucker, Peter F. 1985. *Innovation and Entrepreneurship.* New York: Harper & Row.

Edgerton, Russell 1986. "Quality: The Debate Deepens." *Change*, November/December.

Ferguson, Marilyn 1980. *The Aquarian Conspiracy.* Boston: Houghton Mifflin Co.

Filley, A.C. 1975. *Interpersonal Conflict Resolution.* Glenview, IL: Scott Foresman.

Fletcher, J. 1966. *Situation Ethics.* Philadelphia: The Westminster Press.

Frank, Viktor E. 1959. *Man's Search for Meaning.* Boston: Beacon Press.

Gardner, John W. 1964. *Self-Renewal: The Individual and the Innovative Society.* New York: Harper & Row.

Giamatti, A. Bartlett 1988. *A Free and Ordered Space: The Real World of the University*. New York: W. W. Norton & Company, Inc.

Gibb, Jack 1961. "Defensive Communications." *Journal of Communications*, September.

Gibson, James L., Ivancevich, John M. and Donnelly, Jr., James H. 1985. *Organizations*. 5th ed., Plano, TX: Business Publications.

Guardo, C.G. 1982. "Defining the Mission of a University." *Case Currents*.

Hall, J. 1980. *The Competence Process*. Woodlands, TX: Telemetrics International.

Harris, Thomas A. 1969. *I'm OK — You're OK*. New York: Hearst.

Hayes, James L. 1983. *Memos for Management Leadership*. New York: American Management Associations.

Hershey, P. and Blanchard, K. H. 1977. *Management of Organizational Behavior*. 3rd ed., Englewood Cliffs, NJ: Prentice-Hall.

Hodgetts, Richard M. 1986. *Management*. 4th ed., Orlando: Harcourt, Brace & Jovanovich.

Hummel, Ralph P. 1982. *The Bureaucratic Experience*. 2d ed., New York: St. Martin's Press.

Hrebiniak, Lawrence G. 1978. *Complex Organizations*. New York: West Publishing Company.

Iacocca, Lee 1984. *Iacocca: An Autobiography*. New York: Bantam Books.

Katz, D., and R. L. Kahn 1966. *The Social Psychology of Organizations*. New York: John Wiley & Sons, Inc.

Kunec, J.L. 1982. "Market Your Mission by Stating Your Case." *Fund Raising Management*.

Labovitz, George H., 1980. "Managing Conflict." *Business Horizons*, June.

Lawrence, P. and Lorsch, J. 1969. *Organization and Environment*. Homewood, IL: Richard D. Irwin.

Lodge, George C. 1988. "It's Time for an American Perestroika." *The Atlantic Monthly*, April.

Maslow, A. 1965. *Eupsychian Movement*. Homewood, IL: Richard D. Irwin.

Morris, V.C., 1981. *Deaning: Middle Management in Academe*. Urbana: University of Illinois Press.

Osborn, R. N., Hunt, J. G., and Jauch, L. R. 1980. *Organizational Theory: An Integrated Approach*. New York: John Wiley and Sons.

Peters, Tom 1988. *Thriving on Chaos*. New York: Harper & Row.

Peters, Thomas and Austin, Nancy 1985. *A Passion for Excellence*. New York: Random House.

Peters, Thomas J. and Waterman, Jr., Robert H. 1982. *In Search of Excellence*. New York: Harper & Row.

Pinchot III, Gifford 1986. *Intrapreneuring*. New York: Harper & Row.

Quehl, Gary H. 1988. *Higher Education and the Public Interest: A Report to the Campus*. Washington, D.C.: Council for Advancement and Support of Education.

Robbins, S. P. 1974. *Managing Organizational Conflict*. Englewood Cliffs, NJ: Prentice-Hall.

Ruch, Richard S. and Goodman, Ronald 1983. *Image at the Top*. New York: Macmillan.

Sanford, A. C. 1973. *Human Relations, Theory and Practice*. Columbus, OH: Charles E. Merrill.

3 6 7 8

Schermerhorn, John R., Jr., Hunt, James G. and Osborn, Richard N. 1985. *Managing Organizational Behavior.* 2nd ed., New York: John Wiley & Sons, Inc.

Thomas, K. W. 1976. "Conflict and Conflict Management." In M.D. Dunnette (Ed.), *Handbook of Industrial and Organizational Psychology.* Chicago: Rand-McNally.

Tucker, A. 1981. *Chairing the Academic Department.* Washington, DC: American Council on Education.

Van Fleet, James 1984. *Lifetime Conversation Guide.* Englewood Cliffs, NJ: Prentice-Hall.

Von Oech, Roger 1983. *A Whack on the Side of the Head.* New York: Harper and Row.

Walker, Donald E. 1979. *The Effective Administrator.* San Francisco: Jossey-Bass.

Walton, Mary 1986. *The Deming Management Method.* New York: Putnam Publishing Group.

Whitten, David 1984. "Effective Administrators: Good Management on the College Campus." *Change*, November/December.

Whitehead, Alfred North 1953. *The Aims of Education.* New York: Mentor Books.